CULT
SANDWICHES

Published in 2025 by Welbeck
An Imprint of HEADLINE PUBLISHING GROUP LIMITED

1

Cataloguing in Publication Data is available from the British Library

ISBN 978 1 035 42191 6

Printed and bound in China by RR Donnelley

MIX
Paper | Supporting
responsible forestry
FSC® C104740

Editorial: Isabel Wilkinson / Emma Hanson
Design: Russell Knowles
Production: Rachel Burgess
Picture Research: Paul Langan

HEADLINE PUBLISHING GROUP LIMITED
An Hachette UK Company
Carmelite House
50 Victoria Embankment
London EC4Y 0DZ

The authorised representative in the EEA is Hachette Ireland,
8 Castlecourt Centre, Dublin 15, D15 XTP3, Ireland (email: info@hbgi.ie)

www.headline.co.uk
www.hachette.co.uk

CULT SANDWICHES

the ultimate guide to iconic things-in-bread
from around the world

DAVID PAW

WELBECK

Contents

Introduction

If you've picked up this book, the chances are that you'll already be familiar with many aspects of sandwich culture. Call it the times we live in, but a myriad of factors within the past decade have pushed the humble sandwich to the status of lofty gourmet dish or bucket-list trophy, with every variation under the sun imaginable.

"Will it sandwich?" has become, for those old enough to remember, the new "Will it blend?". The only prerequisite is that it involves two slices of bread and ideally an audience. Having exhausted the options in their city, food bloggers will regularly chase tenuous leads in the suburbs to find the next great thing, a shiny trophy to brandish to their followers and beat the competition to the punch. And many will think nothing of painstakingly embarking upon a multi-step, multi-day recipe for the sake of placing it between two slices of shokupan and livestreaming as they devour their creation within moments before their followers, mukbang-style – and then, hopefully, landing on a stranger's FYP or Explore page.

Yes, internet culture has been a major propellant in creating widespread hysteria around what is essentially a food item that, in its best forms, has almost always been born of opportunism, adaptation, frugality – and necessity. A flagging economy and, earlier, a pandemic required food businesses and restaurants to create new dishes to stay alive, ideally ones that were delicious, economical, portable and, crucially, Instagrammable.

But that isn't to say that many of these engagement-baiting creations have had much lasting power beyond the surge of dopamine that such virality temporarily bestows, and you will find very few of them in this book. As writers and editors, storytelling is at the heart of what we do, and while social media is littered with perfectly edited and visually spectacular creations – get that ASMR of a knife scraping a perfect cheese crust – much rarer is the creator or blogger who takes the time to delve into the story behind each sandwich.

Those stories and histories are, I hope, at the heart of *Cult Sandwiches*, condensed origin stories that tell the story of a place in time, or a neighbourhood, or the context that ushered the ndambé sandwich or a French dip into existence. A discussion about a sandwich's contents and the experience of preparing, buying or consuming it will take you far – but a conversation about the people and the history of that sandwich can lead to infinite possibilities.

Those conversations about the people behind the food we love to eat are also the perfect gateway into a better understanding – not just of what we consume, but also of how a given dish came to be. It shouldn't be a bombshell to anyone that so many great sandwiches were created by immigrants adapting the food and ingredients they brought from home (anything made by

Eastern European Jews, like pastrami or salt beef; or the North African influence in the venerable merguez frites of Paris), but it should be a reminder that what is now considered emblematic or embedded in the identity of a city or people was once considered alien.

So, too, there should be an appreciation and acknowledgement that those under the rule of empires may have been introduced to bread or cheese but it was local innovation and resilience that led to creations beyond the wildest dreams of the average Western European colonizer. Think of the Indian vada pav or Bombay sandwich, not to mention the sandwich-adjacent bunny chow from Durban or, indeed, all-time greats like the Tunisian fricassé or Vietnamese bánh mì.

On the note of bunny chow, each list self-defines its own parameters as to what constitutes a "sandwich". Where does an open-faced sandwich end and a flatbread begin? Is a Colombian arepa a sandwich and if so, what about Taiwanese gua bao? If most people accept lobster and clam rolls as sandwiches, why the resistance to hot dogs? And if a hamburger is one definition of a sandwich, why does it rarely show up on sandwich lists?

The truth is that the sheer commonality of the sandwich, along with the fact that everyone has some claim to being an expert, means that something as everyday and prosaic as this is hard to define – harder, certainly, than the definition of a fundamental force like gravity or the point at which your cardiologist starts prescribing you statins for all of the things you've consumed in the name of research. Most US states can't even agree between themselves – California, for instance, considers both hot dogs and hamburgers to be sandwiches, while Massachusetts and Indiana can't decide on whether a burrito is or not. New York has, however, risked the wrath of the masses by defining anything involving bread as a sandwich.

And while a list of 100 sandwiches outwardly feels comprehensive, the truth is that it would be easy enough to write in-depth about that many sandwiches found in any major city, and a century of sandwiches barely allows for scratching the surface – most of the territory in this book is well trod by real aficionados, and so what constitutes a "sandwich" has already broadly been defined.

Most of us know greatness when we bite into it; the gestalt of the perfect sandwich; skilful manipulation of starch and air and protein, textural synergy, layered harmonies and the perfect ratio of bread to filling.

Which leads me to the home stretch of my preamble. As someone who's spent a large chunk of their adult life making a living by writing about food, I'm often asked: "What's the best sandwich you've ever eaten?" And for all of the doorstop pastrami sandwiches and the bologna specials that light up the memory, or the things between bread which make me yearn for Vietnam or Italy or Spain, the one I crave the most is a simple chicken sandwich from my neighbourhood café. It's got me through the pandemic, a thousand deadlines, and it's been there for me through most of the past decade.

Which is to say, there is no "best" sandwich, save for the one you make at home with the best ingredients you can find, and there is no "best" sandwich shop, except for the ones in your city that take the time to do it right. In food as in life, there's always the next thing that we're endlessly gasping for. Except, sometimes, there doesn't have to be – many wonderful things have always come from that point between necessity and opportunism. And the next thing you decide to put between bread might just be one of them.

Wilensky's Special
(Wilensky's Light Lunch, Montreal)

INGREDIENTS
- kaiser roll
- beef salami
- beef bologna
- yellow mustard

The adage, "the customer is always right" doesn't really hold water at this legendary sandwich counter in Montreal's old Jewish district. The setup at Wilensky's is simple – a few seats at a counter, a short menu, and if you hadn't clocked the sign that says "No substitutions. No changes" as you enter, the proprietors won't hesitate to let you know.

Wilensky's Light Lunch was founded in 1932 by Moe Wilensky, originally as a cigar store that also served light snacks. The sandwich that would become the Wilensky's Special was introduced in 1934 to offer a quick, affordable meal during the Great Depression. Wilensky insisted on serving it his way, with mustard and lightly grilled for the bread to acquire a perfect, crispy exterior, and his customers soon came to love it just as it was.

As it turns out, Wilensky was right. His beef salami and bologna sandwich on a kaiser roll is legendary – layered generously and far more than the sum of its humble building blocks, it's sufficiently well-regarded that plenty of writers

and critics have waxed lyrical about its charms, as much for its simplicity and sheer deliciousness as for the time-warp experience of ordering and eating it.

Today, the setup hasn't changed tremendously – and neither has anything else, from the ownership (it's still family run and owned), to the fact that each soda is made by hand the old-fashioned way, to the recipe for the Special that is unlikely to have changed in almost one hundred years. As well as the sandwich itself, Wilensky's Light Lunch has become a piece of old Montreal's cultural fabric. Found in the Mile End neighbourhood, Wilensky's Light Lunch has remained largely unchanged since its opening, preserving a sense of nostalgia and authenticity. The interior features original decor, including the vintage soda fountain and swivel stools.

A significant aspect of the Wilensky's Special experience is its no-modifications policy. This steadfast approach has fostered a loyal customer base that appreciates the tradition and history behind each sandwich.

Smoked Meat Sandwich
(Schwartz's Deli, Montreal)

INGREDIENTS
- rye bread
- smoked meat
- mustard

Like its more globally renowned cousin pastrami, Canadian smoked meat has a story that encompasses layers of history, expanding and contracting empires, mass migration and community exchange, which have resulted in what's inarguably one of the most cherished comfort foods of our time.

Schwartz's Deli, founded in 1928 by Reuben Schwartz, a Jewish immigrant from Romania, epitomizes the smoked meat sandwich – thick, succulent slices of rose-pink beef brisket, marinated for 10 days and smoked overnight before an all-day steam and being sliced by hand. The meat is bedded down on slices of rye bread and kissed with a smear of yellow mustard. Situated on Boulevard Saint-Laurent, Schwartz's isn't just a deli; it's a holy site for sandwich devotees and scholars of the kosher tradition, with lines that can wrap around the block, even in Montreal's punishing winters.

Transporting Romanian pastramă to the New World, the Romanian Jewish communities that settled in Quebec bumped up against other Eastern European neighbours, bringing about the magical, alchemical spice rub that flavours Montreal smoked meat. Unlike pastrami, it's a smokier, more savoury bite, with a more diverse range of textures owing to the usage of beef brisket in smoked meat (pastrami traditionally favours meat from the beef navel and plate) and the absence of sugar in most seasoning blends.

Culturally, the smoked meat sandwich is Montreal's culinary heritage in edible form. It's a nod to the city's vibrant Jewish community and the way immigrant traditions have become local staples – a fact that remains so across nations and cultures to this day. At Schwartz's, the smoked meat sandwich is an edible passport to Montreal's past, one bite at a time.

The Caesaroni
(Vilda's, Toronto)

INGREDIENTS
- toasted roll • tomato sauce
- shredded mozzarella
- pepperoni • romaine lettuce
- Caesar dressing

The culinary definition of fusion cuisine may have evolved past sushi pizza (a Toronto gem – don't knock it 'til you've tried it) and now includes, well, arguably most of the sandwiches in this book – but really, the only fusion you need to focus on right now is the Caesaroni. It's the result of a fortuitous hook-up between a pepperoni pizza and a Caesar salad, layered inside a toasted roll and ideally eaten immediately. Located in Toronto's trendy Dundas West neighbourhood, Vilda's fits the area to a T with its creative,

seasonally driven sandwiches, a result of owner Zachary Kolomeir's love for bold, eclectic flavours.

The Caesaroni pairs spicy pepperoni with the crisp, tangy freshness of a Caesar salad, and mozzarella cheese adds a creamy note. Meanwhile, slow-simmered tomato sauce marries everything together on a warm, toasted roll. As restaurant towns go, Toronto remains underrated, but shops like Vilda's reflect the playful creativity and irreverence of the people who call it home.

Halibut Sandwich
(White Spot Cafe, Anchorage)

INGREDIENTS
- squishy white bun
- fresh halibut fillet • cheese
- lettuce • tomato
- tartare sauce

As befits a region famed for its seafood, the simple white fish sandwich has been beatified to institution status in Alaska, and its prized halibut – sweet and delicate, with flaky, firm meat – takes centre stage. At the White Spot Cafe, a busy Anchorage establishment founded in 1946, a fillet of the princely fish is breaded and fried to tender perfection, each bite of the crisp exterior revealing pearlescent chunks of halibut. Lettuce

and juicy tomato provide a refreshing contrast, while homemade tartare sauce adds a flavourful, acidic kick, all neatly packed in a toasted bun.

Anchorage, with its unparalleled access to fresh seafood, makes the Halibut Sandwich at the White Spot Cafe a natural choice for locals year-round and out-of-towners come May, when the state's tourism season officially kicks off.

Muffuletta
(Central Grocery, New Orleans)

INGREDIENTS
- seeded Sicilian loaf
- Italian cold cuts
- provolone cheese
- giardiniera

The most memorable sandwiches are often ones irrevocably tied to a time and place, as is the case with the Muffuletta from Central Grocery in New Orleans. It's a delicate bruiser of a sandwich, packing talian cold cuts, cheese and pickles into an enormous round Sicilian loaf.

This iconic New Orleans sandwich was created in the early twentieth century by Salvatore Lupo, a Sicilian immigrant who opened Central Grocery in the French Quarter. Lupo came up with the sandwich in 1906 as a hearty, portable meal for Italian dock workers. Combining a deli's worth of familiar flavours in a convenient, all-in-one package, the Muffuletta was a hit and the rest, as they say, is history.

Start with a seeded round Sicilian loaf – the muffuletta – then generously fill with uniform layers of Italian cold cuts like salami, ham and mortadella, and provolone cheese. Finally, remember the real star – the giardiniera, a delightful, tangy mess of pickled cauliflower, carrots, celery and onions that adds acidic balance and bite. This should be served at room temperature, and ideally left to marinade inside the sandwich before eating so that the flavours mingle effortlessly.

Having survived everything from the COVID-19 pandemic to Hurricane Ida, Central Grocery is today honoured as one of the city's landmark food businesses and an anchor of New Orleans' French Quarter, but remains as down to earth as ever. Meanwhile, the Muffuletta is recognized as one of the city's proudest culinary offerings in a city teeming with them – no mean feat, given New Orleans' reputation as one of the world's great food cities.

More than anything else, the sandwich is a symbol of New Orleans' Italian heritage and its knack for culinary innovation. It's a beloved staple, revered by locals and tourists alike, embodying the city's creativity and pragmatism – just like the people who have made it their home.

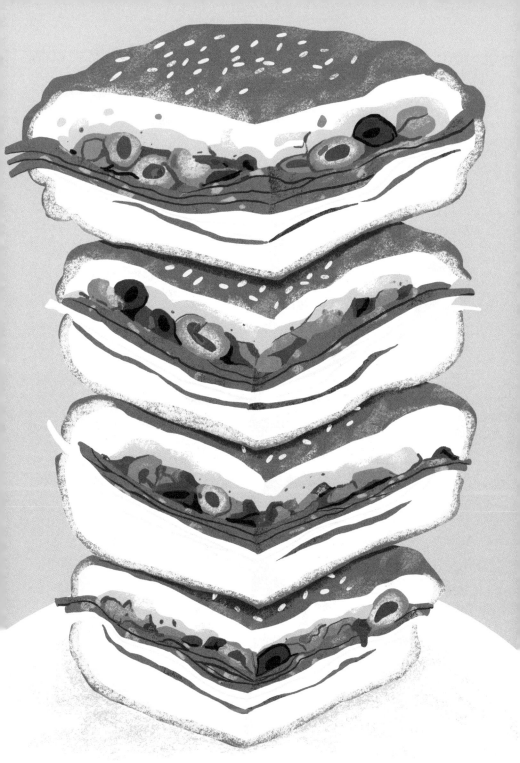

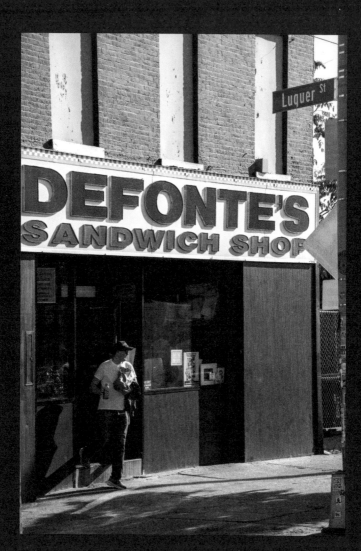

The Golden Boy Sandwich
(Defonte's, NYC)

INGREDIENTS
- white hero roll
- chicken cutlet
- fresh mozzarella
- vodka sauce
- prosciutto

Long before social media adopted sandwiches as a go-to vehicle for inciting a particular kind of food envy, there was Defonte's. Located in Red Hook, Brooklyn, this old-school spot has been a beacon of Italian-American fare since 1922, and a blueprint for many of the city's aspiring sandwich slingers. Established by Nick Defonte, an immigrant from Italy, the eatery became a neighbourhood staple and a popular choice for the longshoremen who worked nearby. Now run by his grandson Nicky, it is known for the house speciality, The Golden Boy, a North Star example of a great sandwich, combining simple, high-quality ingredients in a soft, crusty white hero roll – imagine the succulence of a chicken cutlet and the creaminess of fresh mozzarella mingling with the intense savoury tang of vodka sauce and the lingering note of prosciutto.

As a sandwich, it's a fitting reflection of the city's Southern Italian heritage. Meanwhile, Red Hook, once a gritty industrial area, has gentrified like the rest of Brooklyn, but retains its working-class roots. Far from an anachronism, Defonte's remains a vibrant and important cornerstone of the community, drawing a loyal crowd – from all over the city – that transcends generations. This sandwich encapsulates the Italian-American tradition of turning humble ingredients into something sublime.

Atomic Meatloaf Meltdown
(All Star Sandwich Bar, Boston)

INGREDIENTS
- toasted sourdough
- homemade meatloaf
- spicy Pepper Jack cheese
- red onion jam
- Inner Beauty hot sauce

Their homage to beef on weck (a roast beef sandwich served in a kummelweck, or kaiser roll) may be the popular one at this cosy sandwich bar in Cambridge's busy Inman Square. But the Atomic Meatloaf Meltdown – an inventive, *this one goes to 11* take on the classic meatball melt – is the one that gets the nerds all hot and bothered. Here, thick slices of house-made meatloaf are the star, amplified by fiery Pepper Jack cheese and overtones of chilli heat from Scotch Bonnet peppers and tropical fruit, courtesy of the Bajan hot sauce layered on top. A slick of red onion jam adds delicate sweetness, all layered between toasted sourdough.

The sandwich takes a comfort food classic and transforms it into a culinary adventure, a keen reflection of the shop's iconoclastic ethos. The name may draw you in, but as a meal, it's a reflection of the sandwich's potential as a vehicle for creativity and individualism.

Chopped Cheese
(East Harlem, NYC)

INGREDIENTS
- hero roll • ground beef
- onions • American cheese
- lettuce • tomato • mayo

The mythical Chopped Cheese – a sort of chopped cheeseburger served in a toasted hero roll – has long been a mainstay in East Harlem, where it reputedly originated at the Blue Sky Deli, but took on new levels of fame when Anthony Bourdain repped it in his show *Parts Unknown*, progressively taking on new life as fine dining chefs tried (and failed) to improve it.

But its home turf really exists on social media, where the visual spectacle of its construction (as with any chopped sandwich) and the melty, made-for-TikTok visuals make it irresistible. As a sandwich, what's not to like? Ground beef and onions are cooked and chopped on a flat top, then melded with American cheese and served with lettuce, tomato and mayo on a hero roll. Like the hot dog and halal cart, it's become a symbol of New York's unpretentious street food culture.

Just make sure it's from a bodega.

French Dip
(Los Angeles)

INGREDIENTS
- French roll
- thinly sliced roast beef
- au jus • Swiss cheese or onions

Many things have been invented in Southern California that went on to change the world – Disney, Barbie, McDonald's, *Straight Outta Compton* – but few are as gloriously delicious as the French Dip sandwich, a true Los Angeles original. Picture: thinly sliced roast beef, piled high on a crusty French roll, served with a side of au jus (rich, savoury beef gravy) from a simmering pot for dipping. It's a sandwich that's all about simplicity and flavour, a classic that has stood the test of time.

Philippe's and Cole's, both venerable LA institutions, each lay claim to its creation (though Philippe's has the edge as far as actual historical documentation is concerned). Each has a legion of devoted fans, while maintaining a friendly rivalry. The French Dip has even graced the silver screen, appearing in countless shows and films set in LA. With its unpretentious ingredients and deep, comforting flavours, the French Dip is a testament to LA's culinary ingenuity and appreciation for great food – clean hands be damned.

Tomato Sandwich
(Southern US)

INGREDIENTS
- white bread • tomato (ripe, peak season) • mayo
- salt and pepper

The Tomato Sandwich is a classic, an edible manifestation of the American South's love affair with its summertime bounty. Like the Caprese, it lives and dies on the strength of its primary ingredient – in this case, the ripest, sweetest tomatoes you're able to procure, sliced thick and prostrated on a bed of mayonnaise-slicked soft white bread. A pinch of salt and pepper enhances the flavours, highlighting the natural sweetness and acidity of the tomatoes.

The dish gained widespread popularity in the early twentieth century, a period marked by an increased focus on self-sufficiency and home-grown produce. And, partly due to its deliciousness but sheer simplicity, it's a staple at family gatherings, picnics and church socials during the late summer months. Down South, the Tomato Sandwich is a rite of passage, a seasonal treat that brings with it the nostalgic haze of sun-drenched afternoons, ersatz backyard spritzes and pre-internet, carefree hangs. And we don't know if there's anything better than that.

Collard Melt
(Turkey and the Wolf, New Orleans)

INGREDIENTS
- seeded soft rye bread
- braised collard greens
- thick cut Swiss cheese • butter
- pickled cherry peppers
- Russian dressing • coleslaw

Here's a vegetable-forward sandwich to make the blues disappear, and worth taking time over. Found in New Orleans' Lower Garden District, Turkey and the Wolf, helmed by chef Mason Hereford, is known for its playful takes on Southern classics. The restaurant's Collard Melt is a standout: imagine the crunch of two burnished slices of grilled rye bread melting into tender, flavourful collard greens melded with the mild nuttiness of Swiss cheese, the brightness and crunch of coleslaw and heat from Russian dressing.

As New Orleans culinary icons go, there are plenty – but this is a fitting new-school addition that captures the city's fiercely independent spirit and affection for tradition perfectly. It's a sandwich that reimagines familiar Southern flavours in a fashion that's both nostalgic and innovative, earning itself cult status among sandwich aficionados everywhere.

Chicago Italian Beef
(Chicago)

INGREDIENTS
- sturdy Italian roll • thinly sliced roast beef • giardiniera
- sweet peppers • au jus

As anyone who's unironically captioned an Instagram post or TikTok with "Let It Rip" can attest, the Chicago Italian Beef sandwich is a cornerstone of Windy City cuisine, and its origins can be traced back to the 1920s. Created by Italian immigrants working in the city's meatpacking industry, this legendary sandwich features thinly sliced roast beef, simmered in a savoury au jus (thin beef gravy) until it reaches a sublime, melt-in-your-mouth perfection. It's served on a hearty Italian roll, topped with spicy giardiniera or sweet peppers that cut the richness, and often dunked in the flavourful jus – because who doesn't love a soggy sandwich?

The sandwich recalls the city's rich, ever-evolving immigrant heritage and identity as well as its unpretentious culinary vernacular. Al's Beef and Mr. Beef, two legendary establishments, have been serving North Star versions of the sandwich for decades, each with their fiercely loyal followings. It's a beloved go-to at Cubs games, local diners and family gatherings, reflecting the city's strong sense of community and no-bullshit ethos. Just remember: if your hands aren't dripping, you're doing it wrong.

Cuban Sandwich
(Columbia Restaurant, Tampa)

INGREDIENTS
- crusty white Cuban bread
- ham
- mojo roast pork
- Swiss cheese
- pickles
- yellow mustard

Contrary to its name, the Cuban Sandwich (or Cubano) likely didn't originate in Cuba – that would be the medianoche, from Havana – but rather in South Florida, where cities like Tampa and Key West had sizeable Cuban communities that centred around cigar production. It's one of the finest examples of a great pressed sandwich, long and flat and toasted to perfection in a sandwich press, making use of crusty white Cuban bread that yields after the initial crunch, revealing magical layers of ham, mojo roast pork (pork brined in bitter orange juice for extra tenderness and flavour, and then slow roasted), Swiss cheese, pickles and the all-important yellow mustard.

Perhaps the most famous example is the version from Columbia Restaurant in Ybor City, an institution that's a 15-minute drive from Tampa's downtown area and one of the few remaining relics of the area's boomtown years, when cigar making was a major industry here. Opened in

1905, this palatial establishment is Florida's oldest restaurant and a far cry from the typical mom-and-pop sandwich shop (though it is still family-owned and operated), with multiple dining rooms, acres of foliage and jaw-dropping decor everywhere you turn. But they still serve what's considered one of the original Cuban sandwiches, with the layering that reflects the hodgepodge of cultures unique to Tampa during its rise – Cuban, Spanish, German, Italians and Romanian Jews. It certainly predates Miami – a supposed rival in the sandwich's history.

What makes the sandwich so special? It begins with freshly baked Cuban bread, which Columbia sources from Tampa's La Segunda Central Bakery, itself kicking around in 1915. Their Cubano arrives, plated, with the restaurant's signature 1905 salad. Designed to satisfy without putting you to sleep, it's a sandwich that obeys the law of diminishing returns – less is more – and is good to the last bite.

Fried Seafood Po' Boy
(Domilise's, New Orleans)

INGREDIENTS
- French bread
- grilled or fried seafood
- mayo
- finely shredded lettuce
- pickles

The first thing you encounter when stepping into Domilise's is its owner Joanne Domilise and her team busy at work in the kitchen, assembling sandwiches and preparing orders for their regulars. There's a saying that stepping into a family restaurant is like walking into someone's kitchen, but here it couldn't be more true.

From the outside, Domilise's doesn't look like the kind of establishment that has people dropping everything to visit, even booking a car directly from the airport, but this is a New Orleans landmark, now more than a century old (it opened in 1918). A hand-painted sign outside a yellow house is the only giveaway. Then you step into the dining room, and it's a sea of Formica and wood panelling, with details like a chalkboard menu that's barely changed since 1976.

Its greatest traditions are its Po' Boys: crisp, feathery baguettes with the requisite crunch and softness, loaded to the brim with, usually, roast beef and lashings of gravy, succulent grilled shrimp or crunchy fried oysters. It's then dressed with the addition of mayo and finely shredded lettuce – hold the tomato. This is eating as close combat, as engaging and invigorating as courtside seats at a game six.

The Po' Boy can be traced back to 1929, and a streetcar strike in New Orleans. Bennie and Clovis Martin, former streetcar conductors turned restaurant owners, offered free sandwiches to the striking workers, affectionately calling them "poor boys". Over time, the name was colloquialized to "Po' Boy", and the sandwich became a New Orleans staple.

Joanne follows an illustrious line of owners who have taken the reins of this beloved local establishment. It's built a reputation for exceptional examples of perhaps Louisiana's favourite sandwich but, more importantly, for taking care of each and every person who walks into their establishment. Joanne insists as much, like her famous mother-in-law Dot who ran the restaurant for decades before passing away in 2014. The Po' Boy game is intense in New Orleans, but along with exceptional sandwiches, it's that care and attention to detail that make Domilise's stand out. If that isn't worth dropping everything for, then I don't know what is.

Domilise's

PO·BOY
AND
BAR

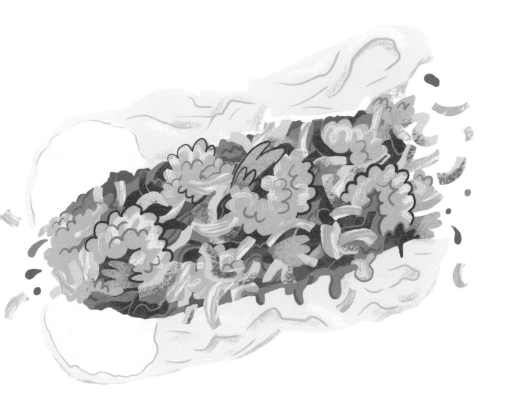

Fresh Mozzarella and Pepper
(M & P Biancamano, Hoboken, New Jersey)

INGREDIENTS
- crusty Italian bread
- fresh mozzarella
- roasted red peppers
- balsamic glaze

When a city holds its own mozzarella festival, you know that it takes its Italian-American heritage and the creamy stuff very, very seriously, and Hoboken's Mutzfest ("mutz" being local patois for mozzarella) also boasts a Sinatra singalong and a cannoli-eating contest alongside all of that incredible, fresh cheese. But what confers local bragging rights is a fiercely contested prize for best mozzarella sandwich, in which M & P Biancamano has trounced the competition for 10 years running.

At this husband-and-wife run deli, there's red-and-white chequerboard on the tables, shelves groaning with Italian specialities, and a sandwich that's won numerous national accolades. The mozzarella and pepper sandwich boasts soft and creamy mutz hand-stretched by owner Peter Biancamano each morning, complemented by the sweet, smoky notes of roasted red peppers. A drizzle of balsamic glaze ties it all together, embraced by crusty Italian bread.

The sandwich embodies the best of Hoboken's Italian-American legacy, and as an homage to Old World flavours, it doesn't get much better.

American Chopped Sandwich
(US)

INGREDIENTS
- sandwich roll
- mixed deli meats
- cheese • lettuce • tomato
- pickles • mayo

Various iterations of the chopped sandwich exist in multiple cultures, but the smorgasbord of assorted deli meats and cheeses at a typical American bodega takes the concept up a notch. Combining a pick-and-mix of deli meats like roast turkey, ham and salami, combined with cheese, lettuce, tomato, pickles and mayo, it's all finely chopped together and served in a sandwich roll.

What the sandwich loses in texture, it more than makes up for in ease of eating and a literal cross section of every flavour – salty, savoury, sweet, tangy, umami – in every single bite. It's a testament to the ingenuity of the American deli, transforming everyday ingredients into something unique, flavourful and endlessly customizable. And with all that hand motion, the glorious excess of piling ingredients high and blitzing them by hand to form an even mixture, it also makes for a great video on social media – an additional, but not necessarily primary, allure of this ingenious sandwich.

"The Sandwich"
(Roma Market, Los Angeles)

INGREDIENTS
- crusty white roll
- mortadella
- capicola
- salami
- provolone cheese
- olive oil

Los Angeles has enjoyed deserved recognition for its culinary excellence, and now ranks as arguably the most exciting city to eat in the United States. But for every lofty tasting menu, there's a neighbourhood spot that's embedded in the fabric of the community where it's based.

In Pasadena lies a gem that's earned a cult following for its unassuming yet spectacular creation: Roma Market. This is a Southern California take on the imported Italian deli, and at the heart of it is the octogenarian proprietor Rosario Mazzeo, who took over the deli-cum-shop from his uncle after the latter established the business in 1946 to serve the area's once-thriving Italian community. Mazzeo claims to not have had a day off in over 70 years and despite his age, still works daily, advising customers and organizing produce.

He invented "The Sandwich" in 1959 to feed his wine merchant, and it is a masterclass in simplicity, featuring layers of high-quality Italian deli meats – mortadella, salami, capicola – and provolone tucked into a crusty, semolina-dusted roll that Mazzeo's cousin bakes fresh each day. Wrapped in pink wax paper and stacked at the counter, it's a steal at $5.50, and remains an LA icon that exemplifies generosity and accessibility in one masterful stroke.

Roma Market's unassuming exterior belies the magic within. In the era of designer supermarkets proffering hyper-oxygenated water for $25 a pop, the shop could be a loveable anachronism, a time warp propelling us to an older, simpler time. It's not uncommon to see lines out the door, filled with customers patiently awaiting their turn.

More than a relic, the shop is a living, breathing testament to old-school hospitality, and the sandwich itself is a reminder that, more often than not, simple is best.

Hot Chicken Sandwich
(Nashville)

INGREDIENTS
- white bread
- hot chicken breast or thigh
- pickles

For a sandwich with such a storied history, the recent popularity of the Nashville Hot Chicken Sandwich is something that food scholars will study for years to come. For the uninitiated, it's a trial by fire – a multi-napkin, *break out the dairy* occasion that won't be forgotten any time soon. And for veterans, it can be an addiction – a searing, endorphin-laced sweat session with the reward of perfectly seasoned, succulent chicken marinated in a cayenne and chilli powder blend so potent it could wake the dead, fried to crisp perfection and sandwiched in soft white bread. Of all the sandwiches in the world, it's the one that flirts most with masochism – and wins every time.

The story is said to begin in the 1930s, with Thornton Prince III. Known for his roving eye, Prince was served a devilishly spicy chicken breakfast by a scorned lover hoping to exact revenge. Instead of wilting under the heat, Prince was smitten, eventually perfecting the recipe. With his brothers, he opened Prince's BBQ Chicken Shack, which begat Prince's Hot Chicken, an institution with a reputation that burns as bright as its spices.

In Nashville, Prince's remains a cornerstone of the city's food scene and still draws lines out of the door to this day, such is the dish's enduring appeal: everyone from faithful locals to out-of-towners looking to experience one of the most singularly potent sandwiches to exist. And despite the recent surge in the dish's popularity among a wider global audience, hot chicken forms an important part of the African-American culinary lexicon, the dish owing its roots to the ingenuity of first the enslaved, who learned to create magic from whatever was available, and then those segregated under Jim Crow laws.

At Prince's or another hotspot like Bolton's or Hattie B's, biting into a Hot Chicken Sandwich is a rite of passage for Nashville locals. It's not just about the meal; it's about embracing a piece of Nashville's fiery soul. So, brace yourself, take a bite, and let the fireworks begin.

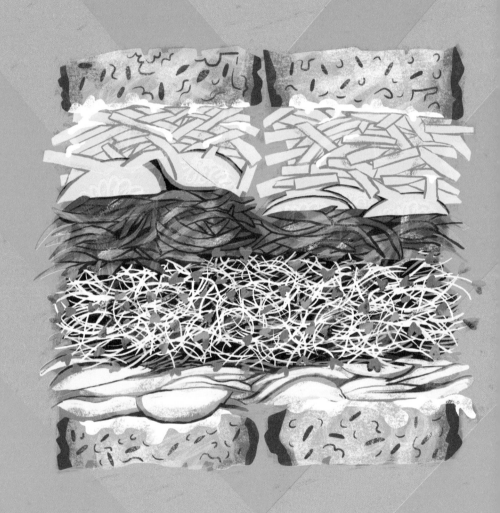

Ira Glass Sandwich
(Wax Paper, LA)

INGREDIENTS
- seeded white bread
- mature Cheddar cheese
- cucumber • pickled and raw onions
- avocado • alfalfa sprouts • garlic aioli

Wax Paper, a cult sandwich shop situated in the artsy enclave of Frogtown along the LA River, was founded by Peter and Lauren Lemos. Their menu, an homage named entirely after NPR radio hosts, includes the Ira Glass – a tribute to the famed host and producer of *This American Life*, and the shop's signature creation. It's a small architectural marvel that balances the salty tang of good Cheddar and pickled onions; the crunch of cucumber and fresh kick of raw onion; creaminess from avocados and garlic aioli – with a mountain of alfalfa sprouts for a verdant earthiness – sandwiched between springy seeded white bread. Each bite is a satisfying cross section of flavours and a textural smorgasbord that begs for another mouthful.

While Los Angeles teems with incredible things between bread – thanks to its burgeoning Mexican and Latin American food scene – the Ira Glass and the shop that created it are resolutely "new" LA, a handheld symbol of contemporary California that, much like its namesake, tells a story with every bite.

Kalua Pork Sandwich
(Oahu)

INGREDIENTS
- Hawaiian sweet roll
- slow-roasted Kalua pork
- cabbage • pineapple slaw

On the sun-drenched shores of Oahu, an appreciation of thoughtful food runs deep, from the luau traditions of Indigenous Hawaiians to the myriad of American and Asian immigrant foods that inform contemporary cuisine today. Few dishes compare, however, to kalua pork, deeply imbued with the flavours of the earth from its slow roast in an underground imu oven, which forms the centre of extravagant luau feasts and feeds everyday Hawaiians via the islands' famed plate lunches.

Piled between pillowy, sweet Hawaiian rolls with crunchy coleslaw, it takes on new life, the interplay of the lush, smoky pork perfectly complemented by the crunch of cabbage and the tang of pineapple that cuts through the pig's richness. In places like Oahu's North Shore, food trucks and local establishments like Kono's have popularized the Kalua Pork Sandwich, turning it into a beloved local favourite and a cherished expression of Hawaii's modern food culture celebrating community, family and the bountiful land and sea.

Pastrami on Rye
(Katz's, NYC & Langer's, LA)

INGREDIENTS
• rye bread • pastrami • mustard

Ah, the Pastrami on Rye. This culinary icon is the edible equivalent of the American Dream – immigration, innovation and, of course, a hefty portion of ambition. Close your eyes and imagine layers of succulent, hand-sliced pastrami, generously marbled with fat and seasoned to perfection, piled high and ensconced snugly between two slices of rye bread, with just a dab of mustard. In its most famous forms, it's the kind of sandwich to make even the most casual of food lovers misty-eyed, a two-fisted endeavour to be lustily wolfed down, manners be damned.

Like smoked meat, its Canadian cousin, pastrami's earliest forms originate with Romanian pastramă, a cured meat made from lamb, pork or mutton (which itself evolved from the Turkish beef pastırma, at a time when Romania was part of the Ottoman Empire). It travelled to the New World in the nineteenth century with Romanian Jews, the majority of whom settled in New York and Montreal. The modern version of pastrami came as a result of different Eastern European communities mixing to create the unique spice rub that gives pastrami its distinctive flavour, alongside the ubiquity of beef in North America.

Opened in 1888, Katz's was the first Jewish-American delicatessen in New York, and remains its most famous. Here, pastrami is cured for weeks, smoked, and then steamed to an unctuous, tender glory. It's truly a doorstop of a sandwich, piled absurdly high and easily enough to feed two, and while the queuing system remains as archaic as ever – a vestige of the deli's working-class roots – the establishment justifiably remains a pilgrimage site for sandwich nerds and deli diehards the world over.

Jump to the other coast, and you'll find Langer's Deli in Los Angeles, which opened its doors in 1947. Founded by Al Langer, this deli offers the famed #19: Pastrami on Rye with Swiss cheese, coleslaw and Russian dressing. Langer's pastrami undergoes a seven-day brining process, resulting in a perfect harmony of fat and lean, layered on seeded bread and delivering an alchemical sweet-smoky flavour alongside the carnal dopamine rush of fat and umami.

Culturally, the Pastrami on Rye is a beacon of Jewish-American heritage, appearing in countless films and TV shows, from *Annie Hall* to *Curb Your Enthusiasm*, and, of course, Meg Ryan's iconic scene in *When Harry Met Sally*, which forever etched Katz's into pop culture. Whether you're in New York or LA – or indeed, if you're lucky enough to be somewhere with a thriving Jewish deli tradition – the perfect pastrami sandwich is the ultimate comfort food: simple, yet deeply satisfying, an initiation into a tradition that's been cherished for generations.

American Bologna Sandwich (US)

INGREDIENTS
- white bread
- thick sliced bologna
- American cheese

Few sandwiches are as workaday, as functionally and stylistically sparse, as the American Bologna Sandwich – baloney to you and me. It's detestable when made carelessly, but a top-tier comfort food when made with care. This is especially so in the American Midwest, where simplicity reigns supreme and artisanal bologna (a distant cousin and evolution of Italian mortadella) is taken very seriously, and regional variations originate from family-run smokehouses and barbecue establishments.

Here, a little TLC goes a long way. At Jamil's in Oklahoma City or Troyer's General Store in Ohio, the Bologna Sandwich is elevated to an art form, sliced thick and griddled to a burnished char, snuggled up with a creamy blanket of American cheese. Far from a relic of childhood nostalgia, a good Bologna Sandwich is succinct and impactful in flavour – and where local delis serve as community hubs, the sandwich is a comforting constant and a cherished reminder of home.

Pho Dip Sandwich (California)

INGREDIENTS
- baguette • thinly sliced beef
- pho broth • bean sprouts • Thai basil
- hoisin sauce

An acceptance of a concept as a whole inevitably means letting in some eccentricities, and there might not be a better example where fusion cuisine is concerned than the Pho Dip Sandwich. A glorious testament to Asian-American culinary ingenuity, the sandwich was born from the food truck scenes of San Francisco and Los Angeles, a permutation of the Angeleno French Dip (see page 21) and a natural offshoot of California's dual blessings of a strong sandwich culture and first-rate Vietnamese restaurants.

Combining the aromatic, deeply savoury flavours of Vietnamese pho and the sturdiness of a French Dip sandwich, this beauty features tender, thinly sliced beef, crisp bean sprouts and fragrant Thai basil, all tucked into a crusty baguette. The real magic happens when you dip it into a steaming bowl of pho broth, transforming each bite into a symphony of flavours, equal parts freshness and comfort. It is, ultimately, a delicious collision of cultures but deeply authentic to the place of its invention – and that's what, surely, fusing cuisines is all about.

BEC
(NYC)

INGREDIENTS

- kaiser roll
- scrambled eggs
- crispy bacon
- melty American cheese

More quintessentially NYC than a yellow taxi, selfies on the Brooklyn Bridge or the lifelong quest to befriend someone with access to a summer house in the Hamptons, the BEC is the breakfast of champions, the New Yorker's morning mantra. If you've ever found yourself needing to fuel a hectic Manhattan morning, you know the drill: fluffy scrambled eggs, crispy bacon and a slice of gooey American cheese, all sandwiched between two halves of a kaiser roll. It's the edible equivalent of a triple-shot espresso, delivering a jolt of joy in sandwich form to start your day.

Our tale begins in the mid-twentieth century, when New York's delis and diners became the sanctuaries for the city's sleep-deprived masses. Breakfast sandwiches were already popular across the ocean in Britain and Ireland, but New Yorkers gave it their own twist, and its popularity and ubiquity boiled down a perfect trifecta of convenience, affordability and pure indulgence.

It quickly became the go-to breakfast for everyone from bleary-eyed office drones to construction workers grabbing a quick bite before a day of hard graft.

There are plenty of plussed-up versions across the city, but really, the best version is the one that's most convenient, and the sandwich can be found literally anywhere that offers breakfast, from bodegas and delis to restaurants and takeaways. Ask for a dash of hot sauce, and watch your sandwich artist at work – who can afford tickets to the theatre these days anyway? Being handed your warm package, wrapped in toasty tin foil, is one of the little pleasures of life in NYC.

Culturally, the BEC is New York's great equalizer. It's the everyman's breakfast, eaten by Wall Street brokers, baristas and buskers alike. You'll see a cross section of New Yorkers clutching their tin-foil-wrapped treasures, each savouring the unmistakable spirit of the city in every bite.

Clam Roll
(Massachusetts)

INGREDIENTS
- hot dog bun • fried clams
- tartare sauce • lemon juice

Originating from the coastal towns of Massachusetts in the early twentieth century, the Clam Roll is as New England as a salty breeze off the Atlantic or a Tom Brady late-game comeback. Imagine golden, crispy fried clams, their briny sweetness encased in a crunchy exterior, snuggled in a buttery, toasted hot dog bun. Top it off with a generous dollop of tartare sauce and a squeeze of fresh lemon, and you've got a sandwich that's pure maritime bliss. (It is, reputedly, even better with an old-school beverage like a can of Moxie.)

These delicious rolls play a starring role at iconic seafood shacks like Woodman's of Essex or the Clam Box in Ipswich, where they've been perfecting the art of fried bivalves for generations. For New Englanders, a good Clam Roll can capture the essence of lazy beach days and family road trips; for everyone else, they're a delicious regional seaside treat that'll have you finally understanding why so many rich people have second homes in that part of the world.

Pit Beef Sandwich
(Baltimore)

INGREDIENTS
- kaiser roll • charcoal-grilled beef
- raw onions
- horseradish sauce, sometimes barbecue sauce or tiger sauce

Baltimore is famous for many things – crabs, Tracy Turnblad, *The Wire* – but really, it deserves some love for its sandwiches. The Pit Beef Sandwich is a regional speciality in the lexicon of East Coast roast beef sandwiches (see also: beef on weck), a simple but delicious creation of roast beef cooked over direct charcoal heat, yielding a flavour profile that's smoky, charred and deeply satisfying – especially when thinly sliced and layered with biting horseradish sauce and raw onions and smothered in a soft kaiser roll. Or try it with tiger sauce – horseradish and mayo.

This method likely has its roots in the city's blue-collar heritage, and renowned establishments like Chaps Pit Beef on Pulaski Highway have turned this local delicacy into a culinary pilgrimage site. Chaps, opened in 1987 by Bob and Donna Creager, has garnered fame and a loyal following. Like the city it originates from, the sandwich is a no-nonsense affair that packs a flavourful punch with each bite.

Kauai Flying Saucer (Hawaii)

INGREDIENTS
- white bread • ground beef
- onions • cheese
- tomato sauce

The Kauai Flying Saucer is Hawaii's love letter to mid-century kitsch, born out of county fairs and school fundraisers in the 1960s. Imagine a sandwich that looks like it crash-landed from the Jetsons' dinner table: a sloppy joe filling (ground beef, onions, cheese and tomato sauce) pressed between two slices of white bread and then pressed again into a circular mould, grilled to golden, UFO perfection. The edges are crisp and crunchy, the centre soft and yielding to a familiar savouriness in the filling.

For many Hawaiians, the Flying Saucer is a throwback to hanabata days – lingo for childhood – and a staple at community events. It's a quirky testament to the island's knack for reinventing comfort food with a playful twist. While it might not have the fame of a loco moco or poke bowl, the Flying Saucer has plenty of devotees. After all, who wouldn't love a sandwich that looks like it could zoom off into space or chase Will Smith through a canyon?

Philly Cheesesteak (Philadelphia)

INGREDIENTS
- hoagie roll • onions
- thinly sliced rib-eye steak
- Cheez Whiz or provolone cheese

The Cheesesteak is as integral to Philadelphia as Stallone or bragging about historical landmarks; as Philly as a Joel Embiid poster dunk or an obsession with soft pretzels. In South Philly, the debate (read: trash talk) between Cheez Whiz and provolone can escalate to levels rivalling your worst arguments with your most racist relative at Christmas.

Pat's and Geno's, two duelling Cheesesteak titans, stand as testaments to this beloved sandwich: The traditional recipe involves paper-thin slices of rib-eye steak, perfectly seared on a flat top, mingled with sweet, caramelized onions.

The pièce de résistance is a generous slather of Cheez Whiz – artisanal nonsense be damned – or melted provolone, all cradled in a soft hoagie roll.

The Cheesesteak is a prime example of the culinary evolution driven by urbanization and immigrant communities, and the Italian-American influence is unmistakable, from the rib-eye's preparation to the provolone cheese. Meanwhile, pop culture has immortalized the sandwich, from *The Fresh Prince of Bel-Air* to *Rocky*. Remember: a proper Cheesesteak experience isn't complete without a messy face and a heap of napkins. Embrace the chaos – it's part of the charm.

Hot Brown
(Kentucky)

INGREDIENTS
• white toast • roast turkey
• bacon • ham • Mornay sauce
• Parmesan cheese

As a genre, the humble turkey sandwich – that workaday meal beloved of office lunch orders – is often overlooked for its sexier European cousins. But the Hot Brown sandwich allows the turkey's succulent meat and buttery flavour to shine. Imagine succulent roast turkey piled on top of thick white toast, adorned with crispy bacon and ham, all smothered in a rich, velvety Mornay sauce. The final flourish? A bubbly Parmesan topping flashed under a hot grill that adds an irresistible golden crust – the open-faced sandwich of dreams.

Invented in Louisville, Kentucky to appease a crowd of late-night partiers at the Brown Hotel, the sandwich became the fuel for the revelry of the Roaring Twenties in the city, which had the hotel at its epicentre. It's an umami bomb designed to soak up the maximum amount of alcohol, an extravagance that reflects the era's indulgence paired with Louisville's appreciation for hearty, comforting fare, and remains a staple on menus across the state today, celebrated in local festivals and beloved in home kitchens.

Monte Cristo Sandwich
(US)

INGREDIENTS
• ham • turkey • Swiss cheese
• bread • egg batter
• powdered sugar • jam

The Monte Cristo Sandwich – a culinary monstrosity that's garnered a following almost purely on the strength of its sheer existence – first graced American menus in the 1930s. It's a cheeky riff on the French croque-monsieur, but with a playfully American twist that Disneyland's Blue Bayou restaurant immortalized in the 1960s. The sandwich consists of layers of ham, turkey and Swiss cheese between slices of bread, then dunked in egg batter and fried until it's a burnished golden brown. As if that weren't enough, it's dusted with icing sugar and served

with a side of jam. The Monte Cristo is one epitome of American excess (the Hot Brown does exist, after all), a brunch staple that doesn't so much laugh in the face of restraint as steal its car and burn its house down. It has achieved cult status, particularly among Disney enthusiasts, who consider it a magical part of the park's experience, but also food nerds who enjoy the novelty of a croque-monsieur and French toast. This sandwich, with its juxtaposition of crispy, sweet, salty and cheesy, is a delightful affront to the palate and indeed, good taste – in the best possible way.

Torta Ahogada
(Guadalajara)

INGREDIENTS
- birote salado bread (or bolillo)
- shredded pork or chicken • refried beans
- onions • mild tomato sauce
- chile árbol de sauce

The Torta Ahogada, which translates to "drowned sandwich", hails from Guadalajara, the capital of the state of Jalisco in Mexico. This sandwich has its origins in the early twentieth century, and it's said that it was accidentally created when a local worker dropped his sandwich into a container of spicy sauce. Rather than tossing it out, he took a serendipitous bite and discovered the delightful combination of flavours and textures.

What sets the Torta Ahogada apart is its robust, spicy sauce and the use of birote salado, the Mexican sourdough unique to the state of Jalisco. The heat of the chile de árbol sauce (with vinegar, cumin, chile de árbol) combines with the tender, deeply savoury pork carnitas to create an explosive flavour profile that's both satisfying and exhilarating. The pickled white onions add a tangy crunch, while the refried beans provide a creamy backdrop. Meanwhile, that *birote salado* is perfect for standing up to a drenching – crunchy on the outside and soft on the inside, it can crucially maintain its texture and tang after repeated dousings. It's served with onion rings, radishes, avocado and chillies and eating one is an immersive experience: it's messy, spicy and addictively delicious, and you may make it through an entire stack of napkins.

While Guadalajara is known for its vibrant culture and rich culinary traditions, the Torta Ahogada is definitely one of its most famous culinary exports. The sandwich is typically enjoyed as a midday meal or a late-night snack, particularly after a night of drinking. Street vendors and small stalls across the city serve up this legendarily spicy delicacy, making it a beloved part of Guadalajara's culinary landscape.

While the traditional torta ahogada is made with pork, variations include fillings like shredded chicken or beef for those who prefer different proteins. Some versions also incorporate additional toppings such as lettuce or radishes for extra crunch. Despite these variations, the essence of the dish remains the same.

Pambazo
(Mexico)

INGREDIENTS
• pambazo bread • guajillo sauce
• potato • refried beans • avocado
• chicken • chorizo • crema

The Pambazo hails from the vibrant streets of Mexico, with as many variations as there are cities. A tumbling extrovert of a sandwich, it may be loaded with fluffy potatoes, salty chorizo, crema and pambazo bread dipped in sun-red guajillo pepper sauce and fried or griddled: it's a multi-napkin affair in the best possible sense. Some variations add sliced avocado for extra richness, while others substitute meat for queso, especially at Lent; Pambazo from Puebla are famous for their mole stuffing, while those from Veracruz are usually paired alone with café lechero.

The sandwich is one of Mexico's thrilling tapestry of sandwiches, apparently named for the Spanish pan basso, meaning "low-quality bread", a nod to its humble beginnings. Over time, it has evolved into a cherished comfort food popular during celebrations and festivals: vendors in neighbourhoods like Coyoacán and Xochimilco have perfected their recipes, making each bite a testament to the ingenuity of Mexico's chefs.

Cemita Poblana
(Puebla)

INGREDIENTS
• sesame seed roll • Milanesa
• avocado • pápalo • queso Oaxaca
• chipotle peppers and sometimes refried beans

Hailing from the Mexican culinary epicentre of Puebla, the Cemita layers just-fried cutlets (the Milanesa), silky and rich avocado, finely shredded queso Oaxaca, chipotle or jalapeno peppers, herbaceous pápalo and a drizzle of oil, all packed into a sesame seed white cemita bun.

Celebrated for its harmonious flavours and contrasting textures, it has won a reputation that has spread beyond Puebla, finding a place in Mexican restaurants and cafés around the world. It's a sandwich that sits at a confluence of local influences and colonial forces which can be characteristic of much Mexican cuisine, from the indigenous pápalo herb to the Spanish-introduced sesame seed roll.

The Cemita's origins date back to the nineteenth century in Puebla, where it was initially embraced by workers who needed a convenient, filling meal on the go. Over time, it evolved into a revered regional speciality, embodying Puebla's rich culinary tradition. The unique cemita bread, with its slightly sweet flavour and sesame seeds, sets this sandwich apart from its counterparts.

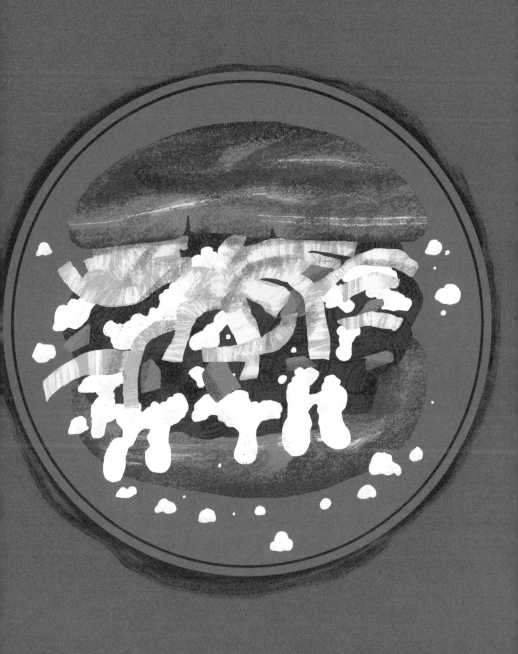

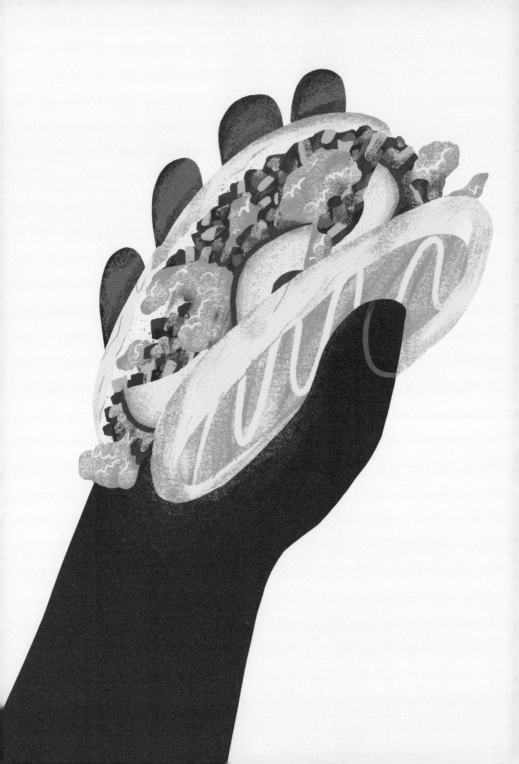

Guacamaya
(León de los Aldama, Mexico)

INGREDIENTS

- bolillo roll • chicharrón
- avocado • pico de gallo
- spicy salsa

The Guacamaya is León de los Aldama's contribution to Mexico's world-class sandwich canon, taking a crusty bolillo roll and stuffing it with crispy chicharrón (fried pork rinds), topped with a generous helping of pico de gallo – tomatoes, onions, coriander – and drizzled with a fiery salsa roja. The crunch of the chicharrón combined with the fresh, zesty salsa and high chilli notes makes for an exhilarating bite, tenderly ensconced by that soft, crispy white roll.

The Guacamaya's history dates back to the early twentieth century, and the streets of León.

Depending on who you ask, the name *Guacamaya* (Spanish for "macaw") is a playful nod to the sandwich's colourful ingredients and extrovert flavour profile, or a reference to the reaction of a customer's reaction when they experienced a bite. It's integral to León's street food culture, a common sight at markets and street corners, enjoyed by locals as a snack or light meal.

Famous spots like Guacamayas Javier and Mercado Aldama regularly draw attention and admiration for their Guacamayas, garnering acclaim with their carefully made, finely tuned offerings.

Tripleta
(Puerto Rico)

INGREDIENTS

- sandwich roll • grilled cubed steak • pernil
- ham • Swiss cheese • lettuce • tomato
- potato sticks • ketchup • mayo

Like many islands, Puerto Rico has a cuisine born out of a history of colonization, the Indigenous Taino influences mixing with the invasive Spanish and the enslaved West Africans they brought to build their society. The resulting culture, mixed with trade and immigration from neighbouring nations, has resulted in a Creole cuisine, of which the island's infamous Tripleta is a prime example.

Enormous both in size and fillings, a single Tripleta can easily feed two – handy, given that it was designed to soak up alcohol after late night revelry

and as a formidable hangover cure. An audacious assembly of three meats cooked over a searing hot plancha – most commonly grilled steak, tender pernil (roast pork) and ham – it layers in Swiss cheese, lettuce, tomato and crunchy potato sticks, adding a final flourish of mayo-kechu (ketchup mayo) just moments before everything is carefully nestled in a soft sandwich roll. The merits of this classic assemblage versus one featuring the Puerto Rican longaniza sausage, chicken and ham are debated, but it's ultimately personal preference.

Elena Ruz
(Cuba)

INGREDIENTS
- soft white bread or Cuban bread
- sliced turkey breast
- cream cheese
- strawberry preserve

There are dishes that are enjoyed by millions – hello, fricassé – but which barely get a mention from websites colonized by the English language. And then there are the less common sandwiches that have small media industries fascinated with the intricacies of their origin story and construction. Such is the case with the Elena Ruz.

But what a charming origin story, rooted in the social elite of 1930s Havana. The sandwich was named after Elena Ruz Valdés-Fauli, a young Cuban socialite who frequented the restaurant El Carmelo. One night, craving something unique, she requested a sandwich made with sliced turkey, cream cheese and strawberry preserve on soft white bread. The combination was so unexpected and delightful that it quickly became a menu staple, eventually taking her name.

Most sandwich origin stories occur out of happy accidents or circumstance, but the glamorous aura of Valdés-Fauli herself dominates this narrative. *Who was she? What did she look like?* The sandwich itself is a savoury-sweet combination not unlike a Christmas leftover situation, the creamy richness of the cream cheese pairing well with the sweetness of the strawberry preserve, while the turkey adds a savoury depth. It's served on rich medianoche bread, and scepticism melts away with the first bite, replaced by the embrace of a comforting and familiar bite that continues to charm those who appreciate the art of unexpected flavour pairings.

Valdés-Fauli passed away in 2011, but though her sandwich is rarely ordered – and now fading from the memories of most young Cubans – it's still important in Cuban restaurants across the diaspora, with offshoots and tributes riffing on the sweet-savoury element and introducing everything from bacon to guava jam. But is it the sandwich that the twenty-something socialite herself ordered?

In the words of her daughter Margarita: "respect the form in which the sandwich was created, and if you do a variation, don't play with the name."

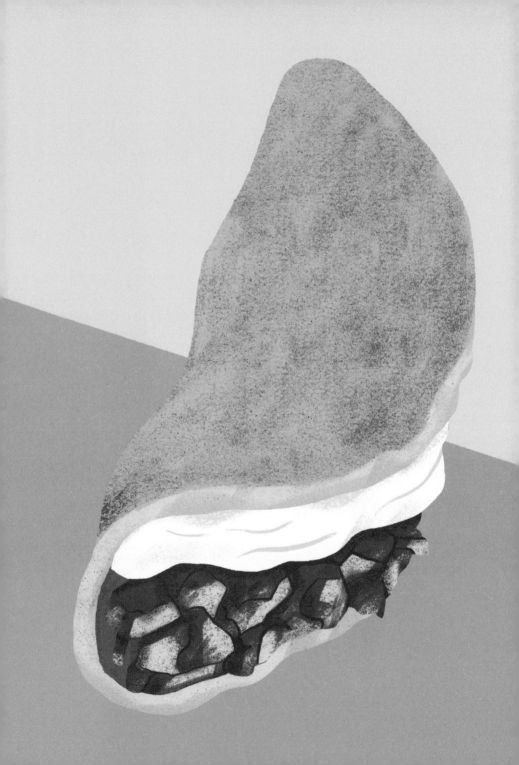

Cachapa
(Cachapera Doña Ines, Caracas)

INGREDIENTS
- sweetcorn pancake
- queso de mano
- pernil or chicken

A folded and griddled sweetcorn pancake encasing salty queso de mano (handmade cheese) and slow-roasted pork (pernil) or chicken, the Cachapa is an everyday treat and cultural icon in Venezuela, best enjoyed from a roadside stand or lovingly made by a relative at family gatherings. Doña Ines and her sons are celebrated for serving one of the best, perfecting the Cachapa's crispy edges and tender, flavourful centre, kicked up a notch by the salty, gooey cheese. And, like many Venezuelan dishes, each boasts a distinct salty-sweet flavour profile that makes it difficult to stop eating.

At her Caracas restaurant, in the suburb of El Hatillo, Ines cuts zero corners and each Cachapa is made by hand, blending fresh sweetcorn, sugar, salt and water. A thick slab of cheese lends depth to each bite, layered with a generous portion of pernil that's been marinated in marjoram and citrus for over 24 hours and roasted in a charcoal oven for hours – but the star of the show are those bounteous, pillowy Cachapas that Caraqueños travel far and wide for.

Bokit
(Guadeloupe)

INGREDIENTS
- deep-fried dough • salt fish or chicken
- lettuce • tomato • cucumber
- hot sauce • garlic sauce

The Bokit is one of Guadeloupe's culinary gems, a puffy fry bread derived from the Caribbean johnnycake – and an exceptional vehicle for filling to create an addictively crisp and yielding sandwich bursting with flavour. It's reflective of the islands' colonial history, with the French violently exploiting the land and native Caribe people to grow sugarcane. The islands' food culture, however, came from the hands of the enslaved Africans who worked in the kitchens. Bestowed flour but without access to ovens, they conjured magic out of nothing and instead fried the dough.

That golden, crisp dough is light and fluffy inside, perfect for filling with salt fish or chicken, salad vegetables and a generous splash of hot and garlic sauces. It's a textural marvel that packs a punch, flavour-wise. Found in bustling markets and roadside stalls, the Bokit is a social affair, telling the story of Guadeloupe's rich, tumultuous history; embodying resilience and culinary ingenuity.

Fish Cutter (Barbados)

INGREDIENTS

• salt bread • fried fish (typically marlin or kingfish) • Bajan seasoning • lettuce • tomato • hot pepper sauce • tartare sauce

Few things aren't immediately upgraded by the addition of hot pepper sauce, and the Fish Cutter is the final form of the fried fish sandwich – a fire-breathing Charizard of a creation that captures the essence of Barbados's coastal cornucopia. It's an iconic sandwich that has roots in the island's fishing traditions: marlin or kingfish, seasoned with a vibrant blend of Bajan spices, is fried until perfectly crispy.

The magic happens when it's tucked into a soft, slightly sweet salt bread roll – a Barbadian speciality and a legacy of the island's colonial past, reflecting Barbados's history of blending African, European and Indigenous influences into a unique culinary patois. Often savoured with a generous drizzle of hot pepper sauce and a smear of tartare sauce, the crisp fish contrasts beautifully with the fresh lettuce and tomato, while the salt bread adds a unique texture and flavour.

The best versions are typically served at bustling spots like Oistins Fish Fry, where music, food and community intertwine and reflect the pace of life on the island.

Fried Fish Sandwich (Bermuda)

INGREDIENTS

• raisin bread • fried fish • tartare sauce • lettuce • tomato • hot sauce

The Bermuda Fried Fish Sandwich is a dish that captures the island's essence in each bite. Particularly at Woody's in Sandys Parish, it's a dish that's achieved an almost mythical status. It begins with the freshest wahoo or snapper, fried to a succulent perfection, then wedged between slices of raisin bread – a culinary juxtaposition that sounds unorthodox but works beautifully.

This sandwich is a culinary oxymoron, balancing sweet and savoury with the dexterity of a tightrope walker. The raisin bread complements the fried fish, while tartare sauce and a dash of hot sauce add layers of tang and heat. Meanwhile, crisp lettuce and ripe tomatoes provide a refreshing crunch. Woody's, a local institution, has made this sandwich an emblem of Bermudian culture.

Historically, the sandwich reflects Bermuda's rich maritime heritage, where fish has always been a staple. The innovative use of raisin bread speaks to the island's resourcefulness and its tradition of blending different culinary influences. This sandwich encapsulates the island's ability to turn the everyday catch into a sublime culinary experience, enjoyed in the casual, communal settings that define Bermudian life.

Bake and Shark
(Trinidad)

If ever there was a sandwich that could embody the spirit of Trinidad, it's the Bake and Shark. Imagine, if you will, freshly caught shark marinated in a clandestine blend of spices, fried to a golden crisp and ensconced in a fluffy, slightly sweet piece of fried dough locally known as bake.

The preparation and enjoyment of Bake and Shark have become something of a cultural ritual, and at Maracas Beach, favourite restaurants like Richard's have cemented the dish's popularity and legend. You'll bite into a sandwich rooted in the island's fishing culture, a riot of of textures and flavours – crisp lettuce, juicy tomato, creamy coleslaw – all doused in tamarind, garlic and hot pepper sauces.

As with so much of the regional cuisines of the Caribbean, it's a sandwich that represents the melding of Indigenous Caribbean ingredients with African and Indian culinary traditions brought by Trinidad's diverse populace. The beachside consumption of this dish, amid the sounds of calypso and soca, reflects the island's communal spirit. It's a gastronomic imperative, a dish that's as much about community as it is about cuisine.

Butifarra
(Peru)

In major cities like Lima and Cusco, the Butifarra is a beloved and revered staple, found in both markets and sangucherías. Key to the sandwich is jamón del país, a Peruvian ham brined and marinated in a blend of herbs and spices before being slow-cooked until tender. The sandwich is classically served on crusty white Peruvian pan francés, a baguette type of bread that that soaks up flavour while maintaining its crunch, and is topped with aji crema and salsa criolla (Creole salsa) – a piquant tangle of onions, lime and coriander with bite from Aji Amarillo chilli. The salsa adds a tangy, spicy kick that dances on your palate, giving another layer of flavour and raises a flavourful pork sandwich into something else entirely.

Here, "criolla" refers to the mix of Indigenous Peruvian, Spanish, African and mestizo cultures that exist in Peru, acting as a positive assertion of self-proclamation that can be expressed in cuisine and cultural practices like music or dance. In the butifarra, it finds a delicious display foundational to daily life in Peru.

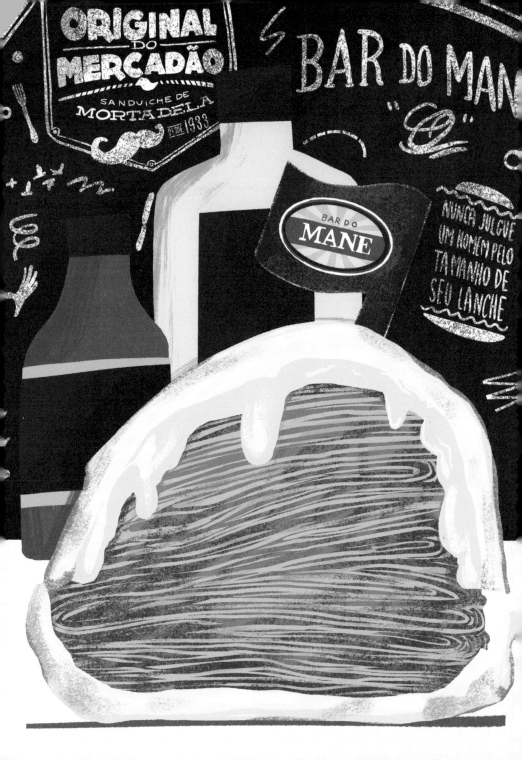

Mortadella Sandwich
(Bar do Mané, Mercado Municipal, São Paulo)

INGREDIENTS
- Portuguese water roll
- mortadella
- provolone cheese

Brazil is famously a dynamic cultural melting pot, and alongside music and dance from West Africa, religion and language via Portugal, and spirituality and knowledge of the land from the nation's myriad Indigenous groups, the Italian faction brought perhaps the greatest gift of them all – cured meats.

The hot Mortadella Sandwich from Bar do Mané, inside São Paulo's frenetic Mercado Municipal, is perhaps the monument to cured meat that we deserve and a nod to the city's Italian heritage. Imagine: a mountain of thinly sliced, griddled mortadella piled high with creamy provolone that melts as soon as it hits the hot pork. It's all encased within a simple white roll that serves as a scaffold for all of that meat (it's said that each sandwich packs around 350g/12oz of mortadella) while adding a much-appreciated crunch to the proceedings. You don't eat a Bar do Mané sandwich so much as swim in it. The sandwich's hearty, no-nonsense nature captures the essence of the Mercado Municipal itself – dynamic, generous and full of flavour.

Beirute
(São Paulo)

INGREDIENTS
- pão sirio • roast beef • lettuce
- tomato • onions • cheese
- a touch of za'atar or other spices

The first Lebanese and Syrian migrants to Brazil arrived in the 1880s, Christians fleeing civil and religious conflict and seeking opportunity, adding to the multilayered tapestry of nationalities and ethnicities still shaping the young nation's identity. Like other sandwiches created by the collision or legacy of consensual (and non-consensual) culinary exchange, the Beirute was born out of circumstance in São Paulo when two Lebanese brothers ran out of bread at their sandwich shop, replacing it with pillowy pão sirio – pitta bread – and adding a sprinkling of za'atar to each portion.

The Beirute of today still uses two pieces of pitta bread – never in the pocket – stuffed with roast beef from Brazil's pampas, lettuce, tomatoes, onions and a thick slab of melted cheese. While za'atar is less common, the bread remains an integral part of the sandwich. It's a culinary portmanteau of Middle Eastern and Brazilian flavours, capturing the essence of São Paulo's eclectic food scene, and an edible historical document of turn-of-the-century globalism.

Choripán
(Argentina)

INGREDIENTS
• white baguette or roll • grilled chorizo
• chimichurri sauce

In Argentina, where asado is the only religion that rivals football, the Choripán reigns supreme. A quintessential street food, this sandwich is simplicity itself: a grilled chorizo sausage, split down the middle, nestled in a crusty baguette or roll, and lavishly adorned with chimichurri – a pungent, herbaceous sauce of parsley, garlic, vinegar and chilli flakes. It's a sandwich that speaks directly to the soul, and to the hungry office worker bunking off work early to grab lunch.

Choripán's roots are embedded in Argentina's asado tradition, a communal barbecue that's as much about companionship as it is about grilling.

For a real deal Choripán experience, Buenos Aires is the place to be. Street vendors, or choripaneros, line the streets of neighbourhoods like San Telmo, their grills sizzling and smoking, drawing crowds with the irresistible aroma of grilling sausages. Nuestra Parrilla is a must-visit, known for its exceptional sausages and lively atmosphere.

Eating a Choripán is a full sensory experience. The sounds of the grill, the camaraderie of sharing a meal, and the rich cultural heritage encapsulated in each bite make it more than just a quick snack.

Gatsby and AK-47
(South Africa)

INGREDIENTS
• Portuguese roll or French loaf • slap chips
• steak • polony • Vienna sausage • Russian sausage • cheese • lettuce • green peppers
• tomato • sauces including mayonnaise, ketchup and atchar pickle

The Gatsby sandwich originated in the 1970s in Cape Town's Athlone district, created by Rashaad Pandy, a fish shop owner who needed to provide a fortifying meal for his workers. This behemoth of a sandwich takes a Portuguese roll and stuffs it with chips, polony (a type of sausage) and a variety of fillings. Similarly, the AK-47 sandwich, a regional Johannesburg variation of the Gatsby so big you could hold it like a gun, is loaded with an excess of various meats, melted cheese and slap chips (soaked in vinegar).

These monstrous sandwiches became popular in the country's takeaways, especially for non-white people, who were forced to rely on takeaways owing to apartheid-era laws that banned them going inside restaurants and erased any time available for the preparation of food.

Today, they remain beloved fixtures in South African street food culture, often shared among friends and family, embodying a spirit of community and resilience, a culinary symbol of resistance if there ever was one.

INGREDIENTS
• hollowed-out white bread loaf
• curry (typically slow-cooked
mutton or butter beans)

Picturesquely located on South Africa's east coast with the warm waters of the Indian Ocean lapping its shores, the city of Durban stands out as one of the world's premier beach cities. At the core of its identity is its large Indian diaspora, many of whom were Gujaratis brought over as indentured labourers by the British, or later as merchants who built their own tight-knit communities.

Named for banias, a merchant class of Indian that arrived in Durban, the Bunny Chow is a capacious, hollowed-out white loaf filled to the brim with a rich, deeply flavoured curry. As for its invention, there are several theories, each emphasizing the ingenuity and portability of the dish. One suggests that it was created for Indian labourers to take their meals to the sugarcane plantations with them, while another reasons that the dish was created for Black, coloured and Indian workers – all of whom were barred from many establishments under apartheid – to take away their meals. Whatever its

origins, the dish caught on during apartheid, and its roots are irrevocably tied to one of the city's darkest eras.

Bunny Chow is Durban's most iconic dish, and, somewhat subversively, has become a favourite staple that transcends segregation. It's designed to be eaten with the hands, and the ritual of breaking bread, scooping out curry and morsels of beans or meat makes it an engaging, delicious feast. As the bread soaks up the curry, each bite becomes a delicious, comforting affair. Originally vegetarian (reflecting the Gujarati diet), it's now commonly served with mutton or lamb curry, chicken or even French fries.

Culturally, Bunny Chow is more than just food; it's a symbol of Durban's rich multicultural tapestry. It reflects the city's Indian heritage and its ability to thrive despite adversity. It's a dish enjoyed by everyone, making it a unifying force in Durban's culinary landscape.

Gateaux Piments (Mauritius)

INGREDIENTS
• bread roll • split pea fritters • chilli
• turmeric • cumin
• coriander • curry leaves

In Mauritius, a perfect breakfast would be a hot, buttered white roll slicked with fresh, crunchy Gateaux Piments and a cup of hot tea. These spicy fritters, prepared from split peas, are an iconic staple of Mauritian cuisine, equally delicious prepared fresh at home or from a market vendor – but always best eaten immediately. Yellow split peas are soaked until tender, ground to a paste, then mixed with green chillies, spring onions, garlic and coriander. Formed into small, round patties, they're deep-fried until golden and crispy, proffering a fiery crunch with each bite.

The story of Gateaux Piments is deeply woven into Mauritius's rich cultural tapestry. This island nation in the Indian Ocean has seen waves of immigrants from India, Africa, France and China, each leaving their indelible mark on its cuisine. The Indian labourers who arrived during British colonization in the nineteenth century brought with them their culinary traditions.

Over time, these traditions blended with local ingredients, giving rise to unique dishes like Gateaux Piments, a symbolic dish that highlights the resilience and adaptability of the Mauritian people.

Hawawshi (Egypt)

INGREDIENTS
• aish baladi • spiced minced meat
• onions • red and green peppers • tomato
• parsley and various spices

Hawawshi is Egypt's answer to the stuffed sandwich and the cousin of the popular Levantine arayes – a quintessential street food typically made from an Egyptian flatbread (aish baladi), filled with a spiced mixture of ground beef or lamb, onions, peppers, and a blend of aromatic spices like cumin, coriander and paprika. Baked until the bread is crispy and the meat is perfectly cooked, it's often enjoyed as a snack or quick meal, typically accompanied by pickles and a squeeze of lemon juice to enhance its rich flavours.

Hawawshi's origins trace back to 1970s Cairo, where Ahmed Hawawshi, a butcher, sought to create a dish that was both hearty and easy to prepare. His creation became wildly popular among the streets and markets of the Egyptian capital, eventually cementing its status as a beloved staple of the nation's street food culture.

Significantly, the dish highlights the influence of various historical periods on Egyptian cuisine, including Ottoman and Middle Eastern culinary traditions, which have left an indelible mark. Today, the sandwich is ubiquitous in Egyptian food culture, found in both upscale neighbourhoods like Zamalek and more traditional areas like Heliopolis. Vendors grill these meat-filled breads over open flames, pulling passers-by into impromptu feasts.

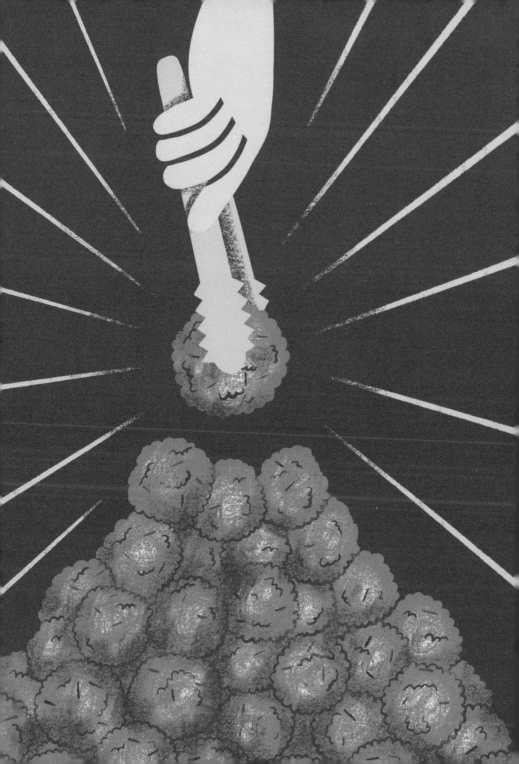

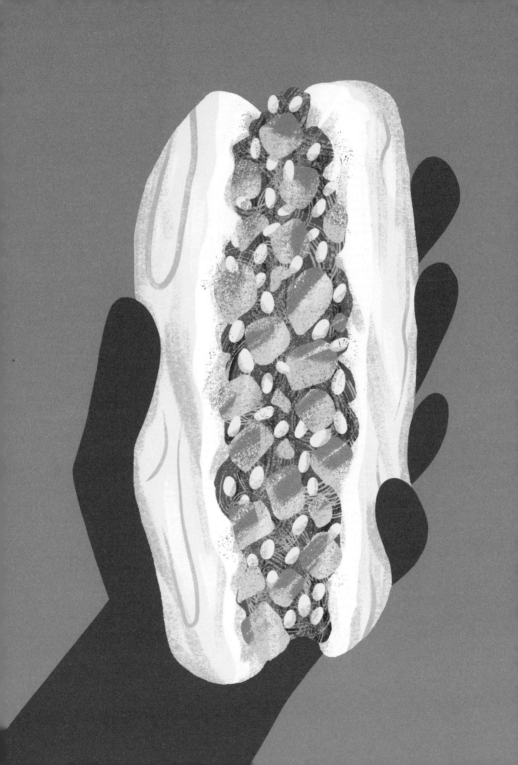

INGREDIENTS
- baguette
- black-eyed peas
- onions
- tomato • potato
- chilli peppers • mustard

The Ndambé Sandwich is an edible reflection of Senegal's layered history. Born in the markets of Dakar, this sandwich fuses French colonial influence with the robust flavours of West Africa. A crusty baguette is stuffed with ndambé, a savoury stew of black-eyed peas, onions, tomatoes, potatoes and a colourful array of spices, including garlic, cumin and chilli. The black-eyes peas are cooked in red palm oil until tender, then slightly mashed, creating a rich, creamy filling that creates a textural counterpoint to the crunch of the bread.

In neighbourhoods like Sandaga and Colobane, where street vendors prepare and sell the sandwiches fresh each day, the dish is a daily staple. They're a common sight at breakfast, providing an affordable and delicious option for locals on the go.

Bridging cultures and histories, the Ndambé Sandwich owes much to Senegal's agricultural heritage: black-eyed peas, brought to West Africa during the transatlantic slave trade, became a cornerstone of the local diet. Owing to the racial hierarchy the French imposed upon the Senegalese, the stew was seen pejoratively as peasant food due to the to the local ingredients used. Now, the dish is becoming a point of pride and a representation of Senegal's proud culinary and agricultural heritage.

To partake in this sandwich is to engage in a cultural narrative that honours both the past and the present, a humble yet profound example of how food can encapsulate history and the enduring spirit of a people, wrapped in tin foil and presented as an act of teranga – the Senegalese cultural gesture of hospitality.

Fricassé
(Tunisia)

INGREDIENTS

- deep-fried doughnut dough roll or soft white sub roll
- good-quality tuna
- black olives
- sliced hard-boiled egg
- harissa
- capers
- sliced boiled potato

Those who have visited the French port city of Marseilles will know the pan bagnat, semi-jokingly referred to as a salade Niçoise (minus French beans) on bread. But it took a trip across the water, to the former French protectorate of Tunisia, for that sandwich to be elevated to its true potential – introducing the Fricassé.

In the bustling, sun-soaked streets of Tunis, the Fricassé combines the bright flavours and yielding textures of that French sandwich – flaky tuna, hard-boiled eggs, briny olives, capers, boiled potatoes – and tosses in the complex heat of Maghreb harissa. Stuffed into a deep-fried savoury doughnut roll and doused with olive oil, it's an everyday treat adopted, improved and assimilated into the Tunisian culinary canon, adored and beloved by all who have experienced it.

Like the bánh mì – a deployment of the baguette beyond a French baker's wildest dreams – the Fricassé has become symbolic of Tunisia's

ingenuity and the ability to take the best of various influences and create something that's utterly, uniquely its own.

One must pay homage to Weld el Haj, a venerable institution in the heart of Tunis's old medina. This busy restaurant has perfected the Fricassé, turning it into a local legend. The rolls are fried to a perfect crispness, while the fillings are prepared with a balance that borders on alchemical. The tuna is savoury, the eggs are creamy, and the harissa brings a heat that is at once fierce and welcoming.

In the realm of global gastronomy, the Fricassé has yet to achieve the fame it deserves, but those in the know understand its significance. To bite into a Fricassé in Tunis is to absorb the atmosphere of its busy streets and everyday traditions, and participate – in some small way – in the sense of community that pervades every bite. This sandwich, with its rich, layered flavours, offers a taste of Tunisia's culinary soul.

Falafel Sandwich (Al Quds, Amman)

INGREDIENTS
- pitta bread • falafel
- tahini • pickles
- tomato • parsley

There are plenty of reasons to visit Jordan, but the one we don't talk about enough is the falafel. On Rainbow Street, Amman's bustling thoroughfare lined with cafés, shop and restaurants, this iconic storefront exerts a gravity that draws everything into its orbit – perhaps it's the pleasing sizzle of falafel frying to perfection in hot oil; the aroma of said falafel tumbling into warm bread with tahini; or the distinctive exterior that hints at its beginnings in the 1960s.

Operated and owned by a father and son duo, Al Quds has become synonymous with the perfect falafel – a crisp, gossamer-thin crunch yielding to a verdant, flavourful interior – stuffed inside warm pitta alongside tangy tahini paste, pickles, fresh tomatoes and parsley. And, like any self-respecting establishment, it makes its own rules – most notably the eschewing of hummus, and the insistence on only offering falafel within a sandwich – but when your food is this good, you've more than earned that right.

Pane e Panelle (Palermo)

INGREDIENTS
- sesame-seeded bread roll
- chickpea flour fritters
- lemon juice • parsley

Stroll through the winding streets of Palermo, and the scent of frying chickpea fritters will inevitably lead you to a panelle vendor. This quintessential Sicilian street food dates back to the Moorish rule of the ninth century, a period that indelibly marked the island's culinary identity. Panelle, made from chickpea flour, are fried until golden and crispy, then tucked into a soft sesame-seeded roll. They're nutty and crisp, and a squeeze of lemon juice and a sprinkle of fresh parsley provide brightness and a final, tangy flourish.

In Palermo's vibrant markets – Vucciria, Ballarò – the Panelle Sandwich is a cheap, delicious feast and a cultural experience combined. It's an everyman meal, beloved by locals who know that the simplest ingredients can yield the most profound flavours, while the sandwich's enduring popularity speaks to Sicily's deep appreciation for street food that's both humble and deeply satisfying. As you bite into a Panelle Sandwich, you're tasting centuries of history and an embodiment of the island's rich, multicultural heritage.

Panino
(Caseificio Borderi, Syracuse, Sicily)

INGREDIENTS

- ciabatta roll
- fresh mozzarella
- tomato
- basil
- olive oil
- prosciutto

"You trust me?"

The bustling market on the island of Ortigia in Syracuse is the place to be on a busy weekday morning, offering the best of the surrounding waters, as well as a rainbow of produce stands – the lushest vegetables imaginable, all ready to be plucked by an enterprising cook. At lunchtime, a line forms at Caseificio Borderi, a legendary sandwich shop known for a Panino that has haunted many a traveller's dreams after experiencing it.

The Borderi family is renowned for their cheese-making prowess, and deploy their homemade mozzarella in each Panino to breathtaking effect. Each sandwich is made to order by owner Andrea Borderi, a master cheesemaker who began selling sandwiches to promote his family's dairy products. He jokes and offers samples throughout the line and sandwich-making process – it's dinner *and* a show.

Borderi favours whatever happens to be in peak season, alongside delights like aubergine jam or smoked ricotta. Caseificio Borderi's prowess, though, is perhaps best exemplified by a simple Caprese incorporating ripe, sweet tomatoes, fragrant basil, a drizzle of high-quality olive oil and salty prosciutto layered into a freshly baked ciabatta roll. A sandwich this simple can work only if each individual component is at its peak, and here, the owners have a knack for sourcing the very best – so as a celebration of the island's bounty, this Panino is difficult to beat.

Panino di Lampredotto
(Florence)

INGREDIENTS
- crusty bun • slow-cooked tripe
- broth • salsa verde

The Lampredotto has been a part of Florence's urban fabric since the Renaissance: imagine the bustling markets where butchers sold every part of the cow and you'll understand how this humble sandwich came to be. The fourth stomach of a cow is simmered to tender perfection in a rich vegetable broth, before being stuffed steaming hot into a crusty bun, then topped with a tangy salsa verde that's a vibrant mix of parsley, garlic, capers and anchovies.

In the Tuscan capital, eating Lampredotto is practically a rite of passage. Found at street stalls like those in San Lorenzo Market, it's cheap, convenient and utterly delicious – a favourite among locals and more adventurous tourists. It's a greasy, glorious mess that you devour standing up, dripping sauce and all.

Caprese
(Bari)

INGREDIENTS
- ciabatta bread • fresh mozzarella
- ripe tomato • basil • olive oil • salt

The Caprese sandwich takes inspiration from the classic Caprese salad and showcases the rich culinary traditions of Southern Italy. Picture this: luscious, creamy mozzarella made that morning; tomatoes so ripe they taste like sunshine; and basil leaves plucked moments before. A drizzle of robust, peppery olive oil and a sprinkle of sea salt ties it all together, all lovingly layered between two slices of perfectly crusty ciabatta bread for crunch.

Bari, a coastal destination known for its bustling markets and deep-rooted food culture, forms the backdrop for the Caprese. Here, Mastro Ciccio has become a local legend, thanks to its dedication to using only the freshest, highest-quality ingredients – as anyone who's experienced a mediocre Caprese sandwich from a supermarket can attest, you really do need each ingredient to be at its best for the combination of flavours to shine. It's easy to execute badly, but when done right, it's the kind of experience that makes you rethink your entire approach to cuisine.

Panino
(I Fratellini, Florence)

INGREDIENTS
- schiacciata • Italian cold cuts
- good quality Italian cheese
- peak season vegetables
- preserved vegetables

In Florence, where every cobblestone whispers tales of the Renaissance and every meal is a potential flirtation with culinary bliss, I Fratellini stands as a shrine to the humble Panino. While there are more famous, more ubiquitous paninoteca in Florence, this literal hole-in-the-wall has barely deviated from its original raison d'être since being founded in 1875, and is beloved of Florentines and visitors alike.

Located on Via dei Cimatori just off the main piazza, this tiny fiaschetteria (informal wine bar) has amassed a cultish fan base that rivals the Medici family in its heyday. There's often a line or small crowd that gathers during the week, but it moves fast – and your Panino and glass of wine might be ready as quickly as the words leave your mouth, with one brother taking orders and pouring drinks while the other assembles each sandwich. It's one of the Tuscan city's most famed

bites, edible keepsakes worth the wait.

The business remains a family-owned one, with brothers Armando and Michele running service each day. Each sandwich comes numbered 1–30, each equally sublime. While time-honoured fillings of prosciutto with goat's cheese or pecorino are predictably superb, try combinations like a popular Panino of meaty tuna with salty capers, salami with artichokes, or wafer-thin slices of mortadella with earthy aubergine. All of this is embraced by freshly baked schiacciata, a Tuscan flatbread that is similar to focaccia and equal parts crunch and chew.

Eating at I Fratellini is like taking a bite out of Florence itself. The emphasis on fresh, local ingredients is a love letter to Tuscany's produce and a reminder of what Italy does so well, while the convivial atmosphere – what's better than enjoying a perfect lunch on the flagstones of a medieval city? – feels like a warm hug from a Tuscan nonna.

Panino di Porchetta
(Er Buchetto, Rome)

INGREDIENTS
- white roll
- porchetta

From Filipino lechon to the kauai pork roasts of Hawaii, and from the venerable lechon asado of Cuba to Cantonese siu yuk, slow roasting a pig is a love language that's common to many cultures across the world, and one of its ultimate expressions finds form at this Roman hole-in-the-wall.

Located near Termini Station, this unassuming eatery has been a temple for swine enthusiasts since 1890. Here, the Panino di Porchetta is a breathtaking melding of flavours: slices of succulent, slow-roasted pork, seasoned with a heady mix of garlic, rosemary, fennel and a chorus of other herbs, all cradled in a crisp, fresh roll.

Er Buchetto's porchetta is prepared with a level of devotion that would make Fellini himself proud. Each porchetta is sourced from the nearby village of Ariccia, in the Castelli Romani, said to prepare the best porchetta in Italy. Meticulously deboned and lavishly seasoned, it is roasted for hours until it reaches a state of porcine perfection – a laborious process that creates a flavour profile which is both rustic and transcendent. Tender, juicy meat encased in gloriously crispy skin, this absolutely is worth the schlep to Rome.

The shop itself is easy to miss, with barely three tables inside plus a counter outside for those insisting on devouring their sandwich at the scene. It is now manned by fifth-generation owner Alessandro Fioravanti, and each slice he offers is the perfect mix of crunchy crackling skin, moist, flavourful meat, and an addictive herbal bouquet. Alessandro is happy to carve a serving of the porchetta sans bread – sacrilege, we know! – but really, the bread itself is simply a vehicle for that sweet, tender meat.

The sandwich is a common sight clutched in the hands of everyone from harried commuters to wide-eyed tourists in the neighbourhood, offering a taste of Rome's famed culinary tradition. Pair it with a cold beer or a glass of local wine, and you've got a quintessential Roman experience that's as timeless as the Colosseum itself.

Truffle Sandwich (Procacci, Florence)

INGREDIENTS
• soft white roll • salt
• truffle cream • truffle slices

Established in 1885, the panino tartufati – Truffle Sandwich – at Procacci in Florence is a classic Florentine snack that reflects the city's – nay, the nation's – adoration of aperitivi, those irresistible, moreish snacks for grazing on, drink in hand after work and before dinner proper. Featuring soft, pillowy white rolls generously spread with aromatic truffle cream made from a blend of black and white truffles, butter, and a touch of salt, the result is an understated, bite-sized indulgence that's as rich and earthy as the Tuscan soil from which the truffles are foraged.

In truth, it's a memorable treat at any time of day, but it's best to mimic the elegant Florentine women who regularly frequent this classic, atmospheric watering hole and enjoy your panino with a glass (or two) of prosecco. About as coveted a luxury ingredient as you can get, truffles have been a part of Italian cuisine for centuries, valued for their heady aroma and flavour. The use of truffles in this sandwich signifies the high regard for quality and luxury in Florentine cuisine, tracing back to the Renaissance period when Florence was a hub of culture and wealth.

Cachorrinho (Gazela, Porto)

INGREDIENTS
• small baguette • spicy hot dog sausage
• melted cheese
• mustard • crispy onions

We're well aware that everyone talks about the francesinha sandwich – that ungodly mess of protein, fat and sauce – when Porto comes up, but often as a culinary trophy in the metaphorical cabinet as opposed to, well, something that people *actually* enjoy. Enter the Cachorrinho, an *any time*, *any place* kind of snack that's widely beloved by locals and visitors alike.

A popular port of call for this plussed-up hot dog – spicy, grilled and topped with melted cheese, a sharp hit of mustard, and a generous sprinkling of crispy onions – is Gazela, a tiny snack bar tucked

away in the city's busy downtown. There's often a line out of the door, its regulars transcending neighbourhoods and social class – at the end of the day, we all just want the spicy hot dog, toasted and cut into snack-size pieces, served with crisp fries and an ice-cold beer.

There's something decadent about pausing the day to feast on this humble snack, and as a culinary institution, it's deserving of a place in the upper tiers. Don't sleep on the Cachorrinho – it's a beloved treat for both locals and tourists, and a bite of Porto's vibrant food culture.

Bifana (Lisbon)

INGREDIENTS
- Portugese roll • slow-cooked pork
- yellow mustard or piri-piri sauce

In Lisbon's sun-dappled streets, where history and modernity dance in harmony, the Bifana stands above all others. A masterwork of simplicity, economy and convenience, it's an edible love letter to Portugal's spectacular culinary heritage.

The bifana consists of thinly sliced pork (usually shank), marinated in garlic, white wine, pork fat and paprika, cooked until tender and juicy and swimming in its own mouth-watering sauce. It's handed to you in a soft Portuguese roll, so give it a squirt of mustard (Savora is ideal) or piri-piri sauce, for sweetness and heat, and you're all set.

Located on the notoriously steep Rua da Madalena in downtown Lisbon, Bifanas do Afonso is widely recognized as one of the city's elite bifana purveyors, if not its very best. This is a tiny tasca (snack bar) with a short menu, and you'll clock the aroma of simmering pork fat, white wine and bay leaf from down the street. While most Lisbon Bifanas opt for grilled pork, this classic establishment opts for an Alentejo-style that's more popular in the Northern city of Porto, with a saucy, messier – but ultimately more flavourful – bite.

Order a sandwich for less than €4 along with a beer or table wine to enjoy, and watch your Bifana being assembled as the meat is carved and the bun swooshed through that rich, deeply savoury sauce. It's an establishment that favours simplicity and speed, a pilgrimage site for greedy epicures looking for a perfect bite, a snack destined to be a blissful segue on a busy day but deserving of the main event.

Sandes de Pernil
(Casa Guedes, Porto)

INGREDIENTS
- Portuguese roll
- slow-roasted pork shoulder
- cheese

There's nothing like the frenetic energy of a Portuguese tasca bar in full flow – the clatter of plates, the pitched hum of chitter-chatter, the olfactory hit of delicious things slow-cooked in aromatics – and few places do it better than Casa Guedes in Porto. It's just moments from the bustling Mercado do Bolhão, and here brothers Cesar and Manuel Guedes have been perfecting their signature dish, the Sandes de Pernil, since the 1980s. Today it has ascended to the ranks of local treasure.

A culinary cornerstone of this most romantic of cities, the Sandes de Pernil captures the essence of Porto's love for robust, flavourful cooking: a crusty white Portuguese roll, lightly toasted, ensconcing succulent, shredded slow-roasted pork shoulder marinated in a secret blend of herbs and spices, topped with a slick of mustard or strong Serra de Estrela cheese. This is not a sandwich that waits for social media – instead, it begs to be devoured while the meat is still hot and the cheese melts to a pleasing mess. Wash it down with a cold beer. Order another.

Montadito de Pringá
(Andalusia)

INGREDIENTS
- crusty white roll
- stewed pork • chorizo
- morcilla • paprika

Few places on the planet have perfected bar food as consummately as Spain, and this Andalusian sandwich is an excellent demonstration of this contribution to the global appetite. One of the most traditional tapas in Seville, this perfect five-bite wonder will have you wiping paprika-infused pork juice from your chin between sips of cold Cruzcampo – and ordering another immediately after you're done.

The Montadito de Pringá is an unashamedly, gloriously porky bite, ladling cocido (stewed meat) – typically pork, chorizo and morcilla (blood sausage) cooked in paprika – along with its cooking juices into a crusty white roll. It's about as flavourful and delicious as you'd imagine (which is to say, very). While its origins can be traced back to the Catholic persecution of Jews in the fourteenth century and Muslims in the sixteenth, the version that graces the city's tapas bars is thankfully less complicated – and about as delicious as you'd expect anything involving the words *slow-cooked*, *pork* and *sandwich* to be.

El Minutejo
(Casa de los Minutejos, Madrid)

INGREDIENTS
- white sandwich bread
- pressed pig's ear
- garlic
- parsley
- hot sauce

"Everything but the squeal" could be the rallying cry of nose-to-tail culinary enthusiasts, except for those who have been creating magic with unglamorous ingredients all along because, well, that's what great cooks have always done. Deep in Madrid's Carabanchel neighbourhood, Casa de los Minutejos offers a throwback culinary experience with its busy, old-time ambience, excellent tapas and hard-to-find dishes.

Chief among the latter is the El Minutejo sandwich, a labour of love crafted by owner Antonio Romero, featuring thinly sliced, pressed pig's ear marinated in garlic and parsley, sandwiched between plain white sandwich bread. As with the pig's ear sandwich at the Big Apple Inn in Mississippi – another sandwich with a cult following – it's a textural marvel left deliberately sparse to allow the glossy crunch of the principal ingredient to shine. A splash of homemade hot sauce is essential, and the sandwiches are light (and cheap) enough to order a few to accompany your wine or beer – this is Spain, after all.

Bocadillo de Calamares
(Madrid)

INGREDIENTS
- crusty baguette
- freshly fried calamari
- lemon juice • aioli

If you're wandering through Madrid's Plaza Mayor, drawn by the intoxicating aroma of fried seafood like a cartoon cat wafting on the breeze, you've likely stumbled upon the Bocadillo de Calamares. As with the best seafood sandwiches, simplicity and execution are key – the best produce available, prepared with care. Here, rings of flour-dusted squid are fried until golden brown, before being tucked into a crusty baguette. The sandwich originated in the mid-twentieth century as a humble food for market workers who needed a hearty, portable meal to sustain them through long hours of labour.

The Bocadillo de Calamares is a staple of Madrid's street food scene, reflecting the city's no-nonsense approach to eating. It's the kind of sandwich that doesn't need complex garnishes because its appeal lies in its simplicity – many locals squeeze a bit of lemon over the top and, if they're feeling particularly extravagant, might add a dollop of aioli. Eating this sandwich is a cultural experience, a nod to the Spanish ethos of savouring simple pleasures.

Jambon Beurre
(Paris)

INGREDIENTS
- baguette
- high-quality butter
- Parisian ham

The everyday ham sandwich takes many forms, including the formidable Spanish boccadillo de jamón ibérico, but arguably the most renowned is Paris's Jambon Beurre, a sandwich that can feel almost audacious in its simplicity. Just a good-quality, crusty baguette, split open and generously smeared with the kind of butter that would make Nigella weep, then layered with thin slices of tender ham. This sandwich grew in popularity in the early twentieth century, coinciding with the rise of the French working class who needed something quick, affordable and delicious to grab on their lunch breaks.

Wander through any arrondissement in Paris and you'll see locals biting into these sandwiches, a reminder that sometimes, less really is more. In a sense, the Jambon Beurre is a cultural artefact, embodying the French dedication to quality ingredients and their disdain for unnecessary accoutrements. It's the culinary equivalent of a little black dress – timeless, chic and effortlessly stylish.

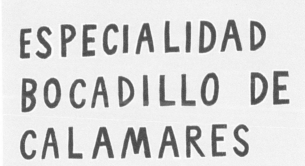

ESPECIALIDAD
BOCADILLO DE
CALAMARES

Merguez Frites
(Paris)

INGREDIENTS

- white baguette
- merguez sausage
- harissa
- French fries

While the jambon beurre may be Paris's best-known sandwich, the Merguez Frites easily rivals it for impact – and beats it for pure thrills. Consisting of a cheap baguette embracing spicy merguez sausages and harissa before being generously stuffed with a pile of crispy, golden fries, it's a handheld feast that captures the multicultural essence of Paris in every decadent bite.

In particular, those smoky lamb sausages are the star of the show, flavoured with fiery harissa, chillies, cumin, coriander and garlic. Their interplay with the crunch and saltiness of the fries is unparalleled in terms of flavour and comfort, while the soft, crunchy baguette is the willing third wheel in this culinary throuple. It's commonly sold at quick-service shops and grills into the wee hours – perfect for soaking up a night's excess, but also just as good while strolling through the city streets.

The backstory of this sandwich is woven into the tapestry of North African immigration to France. Merguez, those fiery red sausages made from lamb or beef, arrived in France with Algerian, Moroccan and Tunisian immigrants in the mid-twentieth century. Like many great dishes, the Merguez Frites is a culinary fusion, a marriage of French stodge with the bold palate of North African cuisine.

While the sandwich is available across Paris, it's most commonly associated with the Belleville and Marais neighbourhoods, both hubs of diversity where global communities comingle and exchange culture. In Le Roi du Couscous or among the bustling street markets, you can witness the creation of this sandwich with an artistry that rivals any trendy bistro.

For anyone exploring Paris, seeking out this spicy, crispy, utterly satisfying sandwich is not just a culinary whim – it's a reminder that, just maybe, cuisine and culture evolve and are never static. So, the next time you find yourself wandering the streets of Paris, eschew the fancy brasseries for a moment, and dive into this local treasure. Thank me later.

Chicken Sarnie
(Mae + Harvey, London)

INGREDIENTS

- sourdough bread
- roast chicken • dried apricot
- celery • mayo • chilli jam
- chives • pickled cucumber

East London's Roman Road Market is one of the city's best-kept secrets, a gentrification-resistant mix of Kurdish, Bangladeshi and Jamaican cultures and one of the few remaining bastions of Cockney London. Founded in 2014 by lifelong East Londoner Natasha Mae Sayliss, Mae + Harvey café has thrived in the close-knit neighbourhood.

The only remaining holdover from the opening menu is Sayliss's beloved roast chicken sarnie, a go-to for locals that combines the comfort of a classic roast chicken sandwich with the lightness of dried fruit, herbs and crunchy pickles. Sandwiched between two slices of hearty sourdough, the entire thing is bound together with the familiar creaminess of mayo and lifted by a slick of chilli jam. As a meal, it's almost impossible to tire of: each bite offers a spectrum of flavours and textures, and, like the café itself, pairs a stylish exterior to a big-hearted generosity inside.

Scallop and Bacon Roll
(Billingsgate Market, London)

INGREDIENTS

- soft white bap
- pan-fried scallops
- crispy bacon • butter

The epicentre of London's fish trade since the sixteenth century, the historic Billingsgate Market attracts a cross section of clientele, who rise early to procure the best of its fresh fish and seafood. Alongside the pros, there are plenty of keen home cooks and, hanging on for dear life, their friends, who almost invariably regret the 4 a.m. start.

All of them convene afterwards at the market's café, which used to go by the name of Piggy's and is a cosy greasy spoon set up to fortify the market's workers. Among the caff fare and seafood breakfasts that showcase Billingsgate's produce, regular visitors know to make a beeline for the café's legendary Scallop and Bacon Roll, a buttered soft white bap smothering smoky bacon and a generous helping of juicy pan-fried scallops. This being old East London, there's nary a shred of lettuce or tomato slice in sight, but this sandwich's strength lies in its simplicity and generosity – and the sense of satisfaction that comes with being one of the few to brave the early start and being rewarded handsomely.

Parmo
(Middlesbrough)

INGREDIENTS
- breaded chicken or pork cutlet
- béchamel sauce • Cheddar cheese

The Parmo is the culinary claim to fame of Middlesbrough (North Yorkshire) and is the kind of comfort food that laughs in the face of moderation. Said to have been invented by Nicos Harris, a former American soldier who brought his culinary skills to Teesside after the Second World War, the Parmo is a decadent, playfully Northern twist on the Italian parmigiana, featuring a breaded chicken or pork cutlet in place of veal, smothered in creamy béchamel sauce and topped with a gooey layer of melted Cheddar cheese flashed under a hot grill.

Commonly found in takeaways across Teesside, this northern speciality is typically served with chips, but is equally delicious served in a simple white burger bun. It's celebrated with an almost religious fervour, complete with annual Parmo awards and fierce debates over who makes the best one. The Parmo is a symbol of Teesside's resilience and hearty spirit, a two-fisted culinary hug – messy, charming and utterly irresistible.

Pie Barm
(Wigan)

INGREDIENTS
- buttered barm cake
- meat pie

Enter the Pie Barm, affectionately known as the "Wigan kebab", a creation that could only come from a town with a wicked Lancastrian sense of humour. This hearty sandwich consists of a meat pie – typically steak and kidney or meat and potato – placed inside a soft, floury barm cake (a type of bread roll). The result is a double-carb delight, best doused with gravy and enjoyed with a can of pop or a hot cup of tea. As a dish, the Pie Barm speaks to the town's hearty culinary traditions and no-nonsense attitude, with its origins rooted in Wigan's working-class history. This was an area known for industry and coal mining, and workers needed robust meals to sustain them through long, labour-intensive days. The Pie Barm combined the convenience of a sandwich with the sustenance of a meat pie, its popularity soaring in the mid-twentieth century.

Since then, the Pie Barm has become a symbol of local pride, a regional speciality that deserves recognition for the terroir that birthed it. It's a fixture at football matches and a beloved post-pub snack, embodying the robust approach to food that defines the region. It's the kind of comfort food that defies the downpours from the Pennines, and can lift spirits in the most trying of times. The Pie Barm exemplifies the Lancastrian spirit: hearty, resilient and unapologetically indulgent.

Smoked Eel Sandwich
(Quo Vadis, London)

INGREDIENTS
- toasted sourdough bread
- smoked eel
- horseradish cream
- pickled onions

There are few sandwiches that benefit from grand settings, but the Smoked Eel Sandwich from Quo Vadis in London is one of them. Located in Soho, the restaurant and members club has been a bastion of British cuisine and good taste since 1926. Today, Scottish chef Jeremy Lee presides over one of the most admired kitchens in London, with a Smoked Eel Sandwich that's equal parts sophisticated and comforting, a joyous nod to the city's culinary heritage.

Silky smoked eel is stacked vertiginously and paired to a sharp horseradish cream and a tangle of pickled onions, encased in two slices of toasted Poilâne sourdough. While we'd happily devour one on the street, there's something about being in his restaurant's dining room – with its lipstick red banquettes, oceans of soft white tablecloths and charming staff – that makes it that much more special.

Ham Salad Sandwich
(Randolfi's, London)

INGREDIENTS
- soft white bread • mayo
- cucumber • tomato
- iceberg lettuce
- salt and pepper
- ham off the bone • cress

Each city has its cultural mainstays that, for some reason or another, have started to fade away, one by one. Think of New York's old-school diners and kosher delis, or Hong Kong's open-air dai pai dong stalls. In London, sandwich shops and delis used to be a common sight, but their numbers have reduced to a fraction of their previous.

In deep East London, by the historic Roman Road Market – a thriving community centred around the shops and cafés that throng a twice-weekly open-air market – that version of an older London still exists, with traditional cobblers, pie and mash shops and old-man pubs sitting side by side with trendy cafés, Indian snack shops and Caribbean takeaways. Anchoring the market is Randolfi's, one of London's few remaining specialist sandwich shops that was set up by two brothers to cater for the market's traders and visitors.

Like Paul Rothe & Son, their more famous London counterpart, the brothers at Randolfi's take care with each and every sandwich they craft – "White or brown?" "Sliced or roll?" "Salt and pepper?" – something to be quietly marvelled at in the Pret and social media era. So laid-back is the café that time slows down when you sit down to eat your Ham Salad sandwich that was just lovingly made in front of you.

That sandwich, while outwardly unremarkable and found in so many shops across Britain, shares so many common traits with more famous sandwiches. They're ingredients that many people would have sitting around in their fridge at this moment, but the care taken in buying the right ham, slicing vegetables to the right thickness, ensuring the temperature of each ingredient is perfect and then actually seasoning the whole lot creates something much greater than the sum of its parts. The freshness and gentle crunch of the vegetables is underpinned by a salty, savoury note from the ham, while the mayo's creaminess and comforting embrace of soft white bread brings it all together.

Very few of the other clientele are under the age of 50, but everyone stops to have a chat, and there's a genuine hospitality to sitting to have a sandwich and cup of tea while peering out at the market. There are shops like it across the UK, but there's only one Randolfi's.

Glasgow Oyster
(Glasgow)

INGREDIENTS
- soft roll
- traditional Scotch pie
- brown sauce

The Glasgow Oyster (or Scotch pie roll) is an institution of the Scottish city, combining two beloved staples into one makeshift, hearty creation. The pie, originally a mainstay for Scotland's working class, boasts a savoury filling of spiced mutton or beef encased in a crisp, buttery crust enhanced by the embrace of a soft, fluffy Mortons bread roll. The University Café, a Glasgow landmark since 1918, is one of the few remaining places offering this ultimate comfort food.

Found in Glasgow's West End, the University Café is a living piece of the city's culinary history, and a beloved landmark that draws a crowd for its traditional decor, no-nonsense approach and comforting cooking. Along with fry-ups and lesser sandwiches, the café serves nostalgia with a side of brown sauce. Here, the Glasgow Oyster features a warm, flavour-packed pie tucked into a soft white roll – simple, hearty and utterly satisfying. Along with a playlist of Frankie Boyle's greatest hits, it's the kind of sandwich that tells you everything you need to know about Glasgow: practical, unpretentious and incredibly delicious.

Grilled Cheese
(Global)

INGREDIENTS
- bread • cheese
- butter

Cheese between buttered bread sounds simple enough, but this is a sandwich that, more than any other, can be transformed by direct heat. In Britain, the cheese toastie has been a staple at caffs for years, while the Welsh rarebit adds mustard to the party. The American Grilled Cheese sandwich rose to prominence in the Great Depression owing to its affordable ingredients, combining simplicity and comfort. And then there are the peerless Colombian arepas con queso and quesadillas from Oaxaca loaded with the region's local cheese.

That simplicity and comfort are key to its appeal, and the nostalgia factor can be exponentially increased by serving it with tomato soup. In London's Borough Market, you'll find one ultimate expression of the toastie at Kappacasein Dairy, loaded with four types of cheese (Ogleshield, Montgomery Cheddar, raclette, Comté) alongside onions and leeks, sandwiched between good sourdough bread and toasted to perfection.

Chicken Fillet Roll
(Ireland)

INGREDIENTS
- soft roll or baguette
- breaded and fried chicken fillet
- lettuce • mayo
- cheese and various sauces

There are many unsung heroes in the convenience store culinary canon (of which, say, the tamago sando, or Japanese egg mayonnaise, on page 119 is just the tip of the iceberg), but few have enjoyed a renaissance quite like Ireland's Chicken Fillet Roll. Born out of the need for quick, hearty sustenance, this sandwich is simplicity incarnate – a golden, breaded chicken fillet, fried to crispy perfection, slung within a soft roll or baguette. Add a basic layer of lettuce and mayonnaise, and you have a staple of Irish life. For those seeking cheap thrills, extras like cheese, sweet chilli sauce or garlic mayo add a further layer of interest.

Found in every Spar and Centra from Dublin to Donegal, it's a lunchtime saviour for a whole spectrum of people, from students cramming for exams to office workers on a break. With the advent of social media, its status as an everyday cultural icon – and for overseas Irish, a reminder of home – has been consolidated through songs and skits. In the land of literary giants and good-natured slagging, the Chicken Fillet Roll is the everyman's feast.

Smørrebrød
(Denmark)

INGREDIENTS
- dark rye bread • butter • varied toppings like pickled herring, liver pâté, cured meats, cheese, eggs and fresh herbs

Smørrebrød, Denmark's open-faced sandwich, is a national culinary icon that traces its origins to the nineteenth century. Initially, these sandwiches were simple lunches for farmers, consisting of leftovers placed on dense, nutrient-rich rye bread. Over time, they evolved into elaborate, artfully arranged meals, proudly served at even the capital's most well-appointed hotels and restaurants. Ida Davidsen, the grande dame of Danish Smørrebrød, dedicated some time and care to transform this humble dish to gourmet status at her legendary Copenhagen establishment that still serves locals and visitors to this day.

Far from the leftover toppings of the earliest iterations of the sandwich, Smørrebrød at Davidsen's fourth generation establishment can range from classics like pickled herring with salty capers and onions, to contemporary riffs like an autumnal liver pâté with crisp bacon and mushrooms that speak to the region's seasons and quality of its natural larder. Whether enjoyed at a cosy café or a formal luncheon, Smørrebrød embodies the essence of Danish dining – elegant, yet grounded in tradition.

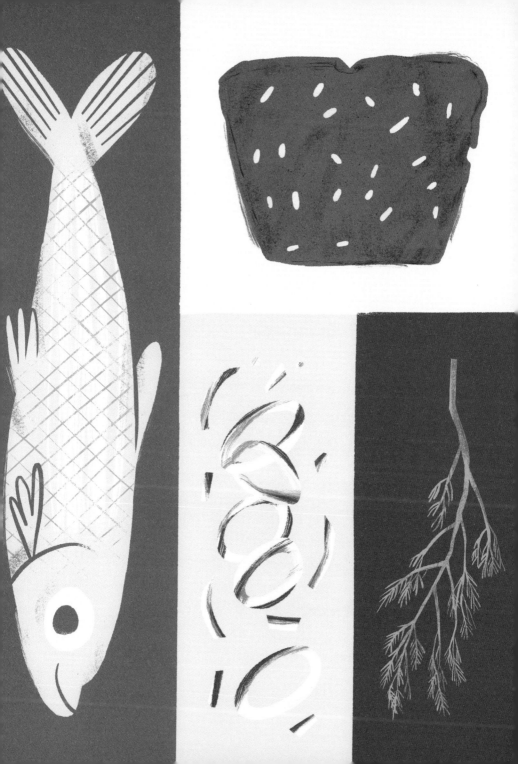

Austrian Finger Sandwich
(Vienna)

INGREDIENTS
• rye bread
• varied toppings such as egg salad
• herring • smoked salmon • pickles

No one does coffeehouse (Kaffeehaus) culture like the Viennese, and the perfect companions to a leisurely coffee are undoubtedly the city's famed Finger Sandwiches. Behold: an array of bite-sized, open-face creations, each meticulously crafted with toppings like creamy egg salad, tangy herring and crisp pickles elegantly arranged on delicate rye bread.

Since 1902, Trzesniewski in Vienna has perfected the art of these sandwiches, and the iconic deli offers some of the best examples in the city. Such coffeehouses were social hubs where intellectuals, artists and everyday people gathered to discuss ideas and enjoy light fare. The sandwiches became a staple in this environment, offering refined – yet accessible – snacks for patrons to graze on. Aside from being delicious, they symbolize the city's commitment to refinement, leisure and community.

Chicken Kebap
(Mustafa's Gemüse Kebap, Berlin)

INGREDIENTS
- freshly baked pitta bread
- marinated chicken • fresh vegetables (tomato, cucumber, lettuce) • grilled peppers • feta cheese
- lemon juice • garlic sauce • chilli sauce

As you exit the U-bahn station at Berlin's Mehringdamm, you're hit with the irresistible aroma of spiced, grilled meat before being greeted by a line of customers. Welcome to Mustafa's, said to be Berlin's best kebab, the people's champion in a city rich with excellent Turkish cuisine.

The Chicken Kebap at Mustafa's Gemüse Kebap is a Berlin institution, but it wasn't always the culinary icon it is today. Named for its founder Mustafa Demir, this modest food stand opened in 2006 in the artsy district of Kreuzberg, a neighbourhood known for its multicultural tapestry and vibrant food scene.

The chicken is marinated and grilled to perfection, maintaining its juiciness and rich taste. The grilled vegetables add a smoky sweetness, while the yoghurt sauce provides a creamy counterpoint. As a dish, it packs a dinner plate's worth of flavours and textures into a portable package that you won't be able to help but wolf down on the street like Saturn devouring his young, horrified onlookers be damned.

Expat food businesses like Mustafa's are tangible evidence of Berlin's melting pot, with Germany being home to the largest Turkish diaspora outside of Turkey. One of the clearest beneficiaries has been the nation's stomach, and Berlin lays claim to the invention of the doner kebab sandwich in 1969. Whether or not this is true, it's become a key location in the dish's evolution, as Kreuzberg's large Turkish community has profoundly influenced the city's palate.

Cevapi
(Balkans)

INGREDIENTS
- flatbread • grilled minced meat • onions
- ajvar • sour cream

In the streets and markets of the Balkans, Cevapi reigns supreme. This culinary relic from the Ottoman Empire is a dish of small, skinless sausages fashioned from minced beef and lamb, generously seasoned with garlic and paprika, then kissed by the flames of a charcoal grill. It's served in a pillowy flatbread – lepinja or somun – and adorned with raw onions, a spoonful of peppery ajvar and a dollop of sour cream.

In Sarajevo's Baščaršija district, the scent of grilling meat creates its own gravity, drawing locals and tourists alike to its vendors. Meanwhile in Belgrade, Cevapi is the heartbeat of Kafana culture – those cosy, dimly lit establishments where time stands still. This daily staple is also enjoyed during festivals, national holidays and family gatherings, each bite a journey through the region's tumultuous history, a portable legacy of the Ottoman influence that shaped the Balkans' foodways.

Kumru
(Turkey)

INGREDIENTS
- sesame sourdough roll • Turkish sausage
- kaşar cheese • salami • tomato
- pickles • mayo or ketchup

In the sun-drenched coastal town of Çeşme on the Aegean Sea, the Kumru sandwich reigns supreme, a workaday titan in the realm of Turkish street food. Kumru, whimsically named after the Turkish word for "dove", might initially suggest something delicate, but this sandwich packs heft. Its origins date back to the early twentieth century when it started as a quick, satisfying meal for local fishermen and labourers. By the 1950s, it had quickly established itself as a treasured staple with locals, and is a fixture today, sold from vendors on nearly every corner.

The Kumru blends influences from Çeşme's storied history. Imagine the spicy, garlicky kick of sizzling, just-griddled sucuk – the sausage that is a nod to the Ottomans – mingling with the savoury richness of salami and the creamy melt of grilled kaşar cheese, Turkey's gift to dairy lovers. Purists may add a slather of mayonnaise or ketchup, but the addition of fresh tomatoes and pickles bring a welcome hit of acidity. In the town's melting pot, ancient Greeks, Romans and Ottoman Turks all left their mark, culminating in this delightful sandwich that merges flavours from different epochs in one harmonious bite.

Balik Ekmek
(Istanbul)

INGREDIENTS
- Turkish bread
- grilled fresh mackerel fillets
- onions • lettuce • lemon juice • salt

Balik Ekmek is Istanbul's answer to that age-old question: *What happens when you combine fresh mackerel with a centuries-old fishing tradition?* You get a sandwich that's beloved by Istanbulites. This sandwich spotlights mackerel grilled on a screamingly hot flat top, served in soft Turkish bread with a colourful salad (lettuce, onions and lemon juice). That lemon and a sprinkle of salt accentuate the flavours, the whole thing collapsing into one harmonious mouthful after another.

This creation has been a staple of Istanbul street food culture since the mid-twentieth century, though its roots go back to the days when Ottoman fishermen grilled their catch on their boats along the river. A quintessential Istanbul dish, Balik Ekmek is as emblematic of the city as the Bosphorus itself – and, not coincidentally, one of the most famous spots to enjoy it is under the Galata Bridge, where multiple vendors vie for the title of the best in the city.

Bun Kabab
(Karachi)

INGREDIENTS
- soft white bun
- spiced vegetable or meat patty
- coriander chutney
- sliced onions

The thriving streets of Karachi in the mid-twentieth century were where vendors first began crafting the Bun Kabab, a culinary cousin of the Western hamburger but with a distinctly Pakistani soul. As the fresh wounds of colonialism began to heal and a new nation emerged, local cooks began crafting kababs with Mughlai-era techniques and flavours, using locally available meat or vegetables melded with aromatic spices – garam masala, cumin, coriander – to create a melt-in-the-mouth patty that sings with flavour.

Typically made with meat (mutton or beef) or vegetables (potatoes and lentils), a kabab is seared on a hot tawa until crispy on the outside and still tender within, before being laid into a soft, buttery toasted bun. Often, it's topped with a fried egg, sliced onions and a vibrant coriander chutney, or a cooling cucumber and yoghurt raita.

Walk down Burns Road, Karachi's most famous culinary street, and you'll encounter smoky stalls, each with their own heavily guarded recipes. The kabab is an egalitarian treat, enjoyed by everyone from schoolchildren to businessmen. It's a popular choice for a quick lunch or late-night snack, found at roadside stalls, food markets and dhabas (roadside restaurants). Each chef adds their unique twist, creating a constellation of variations and making each Bun Kabab a little different.

As a dish, the Bun Kabab has evolved into a cornerstone of Pakistani street food culture and has become a symbol of home for Karachiites across the world. That it resembles a burger may be happenstance – the kabab-burger dichotomy symbolizes the nation's class divide – but as far as delicious things between bread go, it deserves to be up there with the best.

Bombay Sandwich
(Mumbai)

INGREDIENTS
- thick sliced white bread
- salted butter • coriander chutney
- cooked potatoes • cooked beetroot • sliced raw onions
- tomato slices • cucumber slices
- sandwich masala • grated or sliced Cheddar or mozzarella cheese

One of the most popular sandwiches in the world – ask any of the one billion people on the Indian subcontinent who might be familiar with it – the Bombay sandwich is still relatively unknown outside of the country of its creation and the wider Indian diaspora. That's everyone else's loss – this vibrant creation is a showstopper in every sense.

Soft white bread spread with salted butter and vibrant coriander chutney forms the basis for this beauty, layered with cooked potatoes and beetroot, sliced raw onion, tomato, cucumber and pungent sandwich masala. It's finished with a shower of sliced Cheddar or mozzarella before being shoehorned into a toaster until the exterior achieves a gorgeous, burnished brown and the cheese melts and binds the whole mess together. Like the best Indian dishes, it's a riot of textures (the crunch of toasted bread and raw vegetables, the tender surrender of soft, cooked potatoes and the tongue-coating creaminess of cheese) and flavours

(the explosive burst of green chutney, the pungent zing of sandwich masala), which all come together in a harmonious whole that's good to the last bite.

The sandwich is said to have originated from the street vendors of Mumbai, but a better theory is that bread – introduced by the Portuguese via Goa and then by the British – would have been served in sandwiches in Mumbai's colonial clubs, travelling down to the street and reaching new heights of popularity with the availability of ingredients like inexpensive local vegetables, chutney and spices.

Culturally, the Bombay Sandwich is emblematic of Mumbai's evolving tastes, blending diverse influences into something uniquely its own. The vendors who sell sandwiches at legendary spots like Churchgate Station or Raju Sandwich Stall don't just make sandwiches; they perform them, each creation crafted with a flair that would make a magician envious. It's a democratic snack, enjoyed by everyone from busy students to oligarchs.

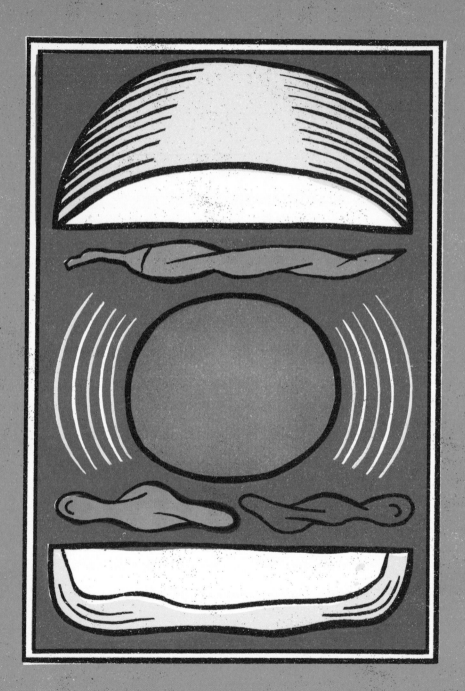

INGREDIENTS
- soft white bread roll
- spicy potato fritter
- coriander and garlic chutney
- chilli powder
- green chilli

On the frenetic streets of Mumbai, the Vada Pav reigns supreme. Lazily dubbed "Mumbai's burger" by the global north, this fiery delight consists of a spicy potato fritter (vada) plucked hot from the fryer and snuggled in a soft bread roll (pav, from the Portuguese pao, meaning "bread"), served with an assortment of chutneys and a chilli pepper.

The Vada Pav's origin story is the stuff of culinary legend. In the 1960s, Ashok Vaidya, a street vendor with a knack for innovation, concocted this snack outside Dadar railway station. Designed as an affordable, portable meal for Mumbai's industrious cotton mill workers, the Vada Pav quickly became a staple because it was easier to eat than the then-ubiquitous potato bhaji and chapati combination on local trains. There are an estimated 20,000 Vada Pav vendors in Mumbai alone, and its popularity and importance to the city's culture and identity can't be overstated.

As a sandwich – and as with most Indian dishes – the simplicity and universality of its appeal belies the complex balance of spices (usually asafoetida, turmeric, green chilli, garlic and mustard seeds), which are added to the boiled potato before it's mashed into pillowy, heavenly comfort and deep-fried. The soft roll – a staple in many parts of India, and the foundation of the sandwich-adjacent pav bhaji – is a willing vehicle for the crunchy, yielding fritter, a glorious slick of green chutney for a spectacular brightness, saltiness and flavour, and red garlic chutney for depth.

One popular vendor for a North Star take on this classic sandwich is Anand Stall near Mithibai College in Vile Parle. Since 1978, this legendary stall has been attracting a diverse crowd, from students to Bollywood stars. Then there's Ashok Vada Pav in Dadar, the sacred ground where this beloved snack was born, where the sandwich's original recipe still wows taste buds and inspires culinary devotion.

Roujiamo
(Xi'an)

INGREDIENTS
- baijimo flatbread
- slow-cooked spiced pork or lamb
- chopped green peppers • coriander

As sandwiches go, the Roujiamo – dubbed the "Chinese hamburger" in the West – has a history dating back to the Qin Dynasty (221–206 BCE), predating the Earl of Sandwich's "invention" of filled bread in 1762 by a casual couple of millennia. It's also reputedly the oldest sandwich in the world, and a staple of Shaanxi province, where it originates. Simple, yet profoundly flavourful, it combines tender, slow-cooked pork or lamb, marinated in cumin and chilli with chopped green peppers and coriander. The whole wet, flavourful mess is then nestled in a freshly baked baijimo

(Chinese flatbread) that's crisp yet soft.

The version at Wang Kui in Xi'an is one of the most famous and remains true to tradition, reflecting the city's rich culinary heritage and rooted in its history as a starting point of the Silk Road. With the advent of social media and a growing Chinese cultural diaspora, this handheld delight is now popular around the world, and it's easy to see why – the Roujiamo blends the Chinese love of punchy flavours with a portable, universal format that transports the eater through centuries of the region's street food heritage.

Corned Beef Egg Sandwich
(Hong Kong)

INGREDIENTS
- soft white bread
- ham or corned beef • butter
- the creamiest scrambled eggs

In the dizzying array of Hong Kong's culinary offerings, the humble Egg Sandwich can get overlooked among the traditional fare. But make no mistake – the Western-influenced dishes at the city's fast-disappearing cha chaan tengs (Hong Kong caffs) are as much a part of the city's cultural heritage as a steaming bowl of prawn noodles.

The sandwich itself is pure simplicity and comfort, relying on consistency, affordability and breathtaking execution for its success. Picture a mound of fluffy, barely scrambled eggs – good enough to rival the swankiest three-star restaurant – coddled between two slices of soft white bread or toast, striking the perfect balance between soft and crispy. A slice of ham or corned beef is a delicious final touch that nudges the decadent to sublime. This is a breakfast that has fuelled generations.

In the aftermath of the Second World War, Hong Kong, recovering from the ravages of war, saw an influx of immigrants and a boom in affordable dining options. Enter the cha chaan tengs – literally, "tea restaurants" that offered a comforting mix of Western and Chinese dishes at prices that wouldn't break the bank. The Corned Beef Egg Sandwich emerged from this culinary melting pot, a fusion of British corned beef and Chinese ingenuity.

For the classical experience, many venture to the Australia Dairy Company in Jordan, Kowloon. Named for its owner, who had worked on an Australian dairy farm, this frenetic caff is the epitome of Hong Kong's casual dining culture. Established in 1970, it's renowned for its brisk service – blink, and you'll miss your turn – and its impeccable comfort food. Here, the sandwich achieves near-mythic status. The eggs are scrambled to a creamy perfection, teetering on the edge of runny, while the corned beef adds a savoury, umami punch.

If cha chaan teng culture is a living, breathing example of culinary fusion and ingenuity, then this sandwich is one of its prized gems, a symbol of Hong Kong's resilience and adaptability, embodying the city's ability to meld disparate influences into something uniquely its own.

INGREDIENTS
• papo seco
• fried bone-in pork chop

Many cultures find common ground in the objective deliciousness of pork. Across its regions, China's pork cookery is legendary – perhaps the best in the world, rivalled only by the reverence for the pig across the Iberian peninsula.

The Macanese Pork Chop Bun, then, is perhaps the logical culinary end point of these cultures, a post-colonial dish that combines a succulent, bone-in pork chop, marinated in a heady blend of Chinese soy sauce, garlic and a dash of kitchen magic, then fried to golden perfection. It's cradled in a fluffy yet slightly crispy Portuguese bun (papo seco), making each bite a delightful contrast of textures while centring the melt-in-the-mouth tenderness and flavour of the pork.

The quintessential portable porcine experience takes place at Tai Lei Loi Kei, a beloved Macau joint, where the aroma of freshly fried pork chops in that intoxicating marinade hits you down the street,

often before you clock the queue snaking out of the door. It was established in 1968 as a modest stall by founder Cheung Kou Kei, who envisioned a sandwich that encapsulated the diverse flavours of Macau in a portable, handheld feast. Fast-forward a few decades, and Tai Lei Loi Kei has evolved from a small stall into a beloved restaurant with multiple sites across the world, and the Pork Chop Bun at the heart of its menu.

Macau's unique culinary landscape is shaped by its history as once being under the colonial rule of Portugal, blending Chinese and Portuguese influences often seamlessly. The Pork Chop Bun is a perfect embodiment of this cultural mashup. The Pork Chop Bun, reminiscent of Portuguese bifana, is seasoned with distinctly Chinese flavours, creating a harmonious marriage that's quintessentially Macanese, transcending its humble beginnings to become a cultural touchstone.

Khao Jee Pâté
(Laos)

INGREDIENTS
• Lao baguette • pâté • pork floss
• sliced ham or pork
• coriander • jeow som

In the bustling morning markets of Vientiane, like Talat Sao, Khao Jee Pâté is a breakfast ritual. Like its cousins, the Vietnamese bánh mì and Cambodian num pang, bread and charcuterie in Laos are the legacy of French colonizers in the former Indochina.

Similar to bánh mì, the crisp, chewy baguettes take a flour base and are baked to perfection, before being loaded with earthy pâté, julienned pickles (carrots and daikon) and herbs. Khao Jee

Pâté additionally benefits from the addition of Lao-style sausage, pork floss and jeow som, the explosive local chilli sauce. Each bite is a breathtaking journey through myriad textures and flavours, balances and contrasts; the flake and hard crunch of bread and vegetables, the brightness of herbs and the high-low treble and bass of that chilli sauce and pâté, and the meaty umami of the pork sausage.

Roti John
(Malaysia)

INGREDIENTS
• baguette or long bread roll
• minced meat • eggs • onions
• chilli sauce • mayo

In one of the most breathtaking street food cultures in the world, Roti John is a colourful fusion of Malaysian and Western staples. In the night markets of Kuala Lumpur's Jalan Alor or Penang's Gurney Drive, it's a staple. Vendors put on a show, grilling the meat and eggs right before your eyes, the aromas practically dragging you in by the nose.

This sandwich features a long, soft baguette spread with a mixture of minced meat – usually chicken or

beef – onions and eggs. The filled baguette is then fried on a griddle until the eggs are set and the bread is crispy and golden. A drizzle of chilli sauce, mayonnaise and sometimes ketchup complete the trick.

Especially favoured during Ramadan, the sandwich provides a hearty and satisfying meal for breaking fast. It's a hearty, spicy snack that's as theatrical as it is tasty. More than a meal, it's a performance, a Malaysian Broadway show that you can eat.

Bánh Mì
(Vietnam)

INGREDIENTS
• crusty baguette • homemade mayo
• pickled cucumber and carrot
• pâté • cold cuts • coriander
• Maggi seasoning • chilli

In the sandwich world, the Vietnamese Bánh Mì has few peers. Take a crisp baguette, slicked with homemade mayo and pâté, and layer pickled cucumbers, carrot and cold cuts with a flourish of coriander and chilli and a dash of Maggi seasoning, then bite into it – a good one is like being granted an audience with God, a mellifluous orgy of complementary flavours, aromas and textures working as one.

The association with French colonialism is widely known – along with crusty baguettes, pâté and charcuterie, the French also brought along mayonnaise and vegetables like carrots – but until the First World War, Western ingredients and food were a tool for maintaining the colonial hierarchy over the colonized Vietnamese – there was even an adage, "bread and meat make us strong, rice and fish keep them weak."

Consecutive world wars disrupted enough supply routes to ensure that French ingredients became accessible – and crucially, affordable – to Vietnamese and vice versa, but the modern Bánh Mì as we know it today was created by the Le family at their Saigon shop, Hoà Mã. Having fled the North to South Vietnam, the family made crucial tweaks to the then-common mode of consuming the ingredients separately, layering everything into a modified baguette (making it cheaper and portable) and adding vegetables to create a filling, delicious sandwich that workers could eat on the go.

Today, the Bánh Mì's immense popularity across the world has bolstered the success of traders back in Vietnam, while a younger generation looks to move on from the ubiquitous street cart model that their forebears perfected – food and culture are never static, after all. While variations of the sandwich abound – filled with fried catfish, omelette, meatballs and the like – the one most diehards gravitate towards remains the đặc biệt, the special or "the one with everything".

Whether you're savouring Bánh Mì in the busy alleys of Saigon, or from a joint in Melbourne or a neighbourhood café in London, it is a delicious journey through Vietnam's rich cultural tapestry. The colonists could never have come up with something this good – it's a story, a revolution and a love letter to resilience and flavour.

INGREDIENTS
- shokupan
- pork or chicken katsu
- shredded cabbage
- Bulldog tonkatsu sauce
- Kewpie mayo

The Katsu Sando is a sandwich that takes a simple concept and elevates it to a focused, incredible crescendo, all while delivering a knockout punch to your taste buds. A thick, juicy pork cutlet (classically a pork chop) is the starting point, coated in fresh panko breadcrumbs and fried to golden, crispy perfection. It's then ensconced between two slices of shokupan (the softest, pillowy milk bread). Add a drizzle of tangy tonkatsu sauce and a lick of Kewpie mayo and you have the Katsu Sando, an iconic sandwich that takes a few quality ingredients and spins them into something greater than the sum of its parts.

The origins of this revered Japanese sandwich can be traced back to the early twentieth century, when Japan was embracing Western influences during the Meiji Restoration. Apparently inspired by a French recipe for côtelette de veau (veal cutlet), the Japanese crafted katsuretsu and later tonkatsu – a breaded pork cutlet that quickly became a staple. Its first evolution into a sandwich came at the tonkatsu shop Isen in Tokyo, when the general manager sandwiched the beloved crispy pork cutlet between bread and sliced off the crusts to appeal to the many geishas who worked in the area, so as not to smear their lipstick.

While it's now ubiquitous in sandwich form in Japanese konbini (convenience stores) as well as on high-end restaurant menus, Maisen in Tokyo is perhaps the most hallowed ground for Katsu Sando aficionados. Situated in a former public bathhouse in the chic Aoyama district, Maisen has been dishing out its legendary Katsu Sandos since the 1960s. Their version features a pork cutlet so tender it practically melts in your mouth, perfectly balanced by the sweetness of their house-made tonkatsu sauce.

The Katsu Sando has also found a special place in Japan's business culture. It's a staple in ekiben (station bento boxes), making it a convenient and satisfying meal for the throngs of busy commuters. Its popularity has even transcended Japan's borders: numerous international restaurants offer their own takes on this classic, from Konbi in Los Angeles and Golden Diner in New York, to the viral sensation that is the Iberico Katsu Sando from TÓU in London.

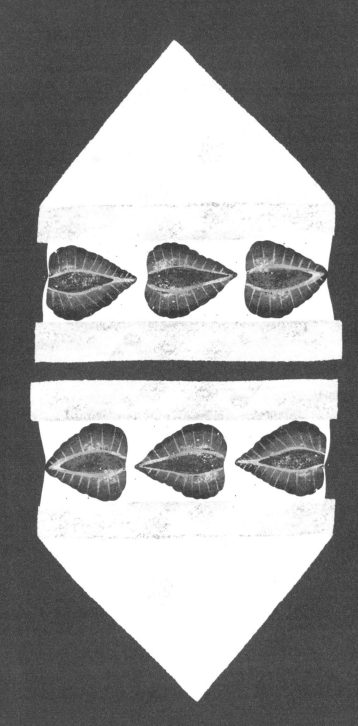

Ichigo Sando
(Japan)

INGREDIENTS
- soft white bread
- whipped cream
- fresh strawberries

The Ichigo Sando is a delightful Japanese innovation that emerged in the early twentieth century as fruit became more accessible during the Taishō era. Even in the whimsical world of Japanese confectionery, it stands out as a charming, pastel-hued marvel. Imagine biting into a soft, pillowy shokupan, generously filled with lightly sweetened whipped cream and vibrant, juicy strawberries. The bread's soft texture, paired with the lush cream and tart-sweet berries, creates an eating experience both comforting and sublime.

In Japan, the boundary between food and craft frequently blurs, and the dedication to daily improvement is a tangible way of life; the Ichigo Sando pays tribute to this philosophy. It was first created to showcase the perfection of the nation's strawberries: establishments like the historic Sembikiya in Tokyo have been offering exquisite fruit-based desserts since the late 1800s, long before the sando found its way into bakeries and convenience stores nationwide. It's also a favourite during hanami (cherry blossom viewing) or as a charming treat or gift to lift the spirits of a friend or loved one. Each bite is a reminder of Japan's meticulous culinary standards, and the worthy pursuit of finding the beauty in simplicity.

Tamago Sando
(Japan)

INGREDIENTS
- soft white bread
- creamy egg salad

There's a reason so many chefs and food lovers dream about visiting Japan to eat, and the lofty standards apply to even the simplest of items. The Japanese egg sandwich, or Tamago Sando, has found its way into the hearts (and lunchboxes) of Japan since the 1980s. This sandwich features impossibly soft white bread cradling a luscious egg salad made with perfectly mashed boiled eggs and Kewpie mayonnaise, a Japanese favourite (and a cult condiment beloved of chefs the world over).

Adapted from a Western concept, the sandwich has been perfected by Japanese konbini (convenience stores) like Lawson or 7-Eleven – and thanks to their pristine, neatly packaged offerings, it's now ubiquitous. Aside from being a delicious, convenient snack, it reflects Japan's approach to food – simplicity, quality and meticulous attention to detail.

In places like Kyoto's Songbird Coffee, the humble Tamago Sando is tweaked to gourmet status, showing its versatility and enduring appeal.

Mie Goreng Toastie
(Dutch Smuggler, Sydney)

INGREDIENTS
- white bread (semi-white sourdough)
- Indomie stir-fried noodles
- cheese • fried egg • sriracha mayo
- kecap manis • fried shallots and spring onions
- coriander

Since the rise to ubiquity of instant ramen and sliced bread in diets across the planet, a melding of the two has been all but inevitable. In Sydney, the café Dutch Smuggler treats both humble staples with the respect they deserve, creating magic with the now-cult Mie Goreng Toastie, an audacious blend of Southeast Asian street food and Australian café culture that its principal metropolises excel at. Here, this sandwich has carved out its own niche, transforming a beloved Indonesian classic into a portable, toasted flavour bomb.

Mie goreng, the ubiquitous Indonesian fried noodle dish, has been an easy hit in Australia, thanks to its comforting flavours and the Indonesian communities who brought their culinary traditions with them. The sandwich combines spicy-sweet comfort via the noodles, a rich, umami embrace

in fried egg and oozy melted cheese, brightness from coriander, and sriracha mayo for a spicy, tangy kick that binds it all together. It's all layered between buttered and carefully toasted semi-white sourdough bread for a satisfying crunch.

Originally created for the café's arrival in Sydney's CBD in 2017, it quickly went viral and earned a permanent spot on the menu. Later, new owner Albert Agus saw the potential to plus-up the sandwich when he acquired the café in 2020, adding spring onion, shallots and kecap manis (sweet soy sauce) to boost its already heady Indonesian flavour profile. More than just a viral hit though, the sandwich is a statement about the beauty of culinary cross-pollination, and has become a delicious emblem of how food can playfully transcend borders and traditions.

Pork Sausage Bánh Mì
(Ca Com, Melbourne)

INGREDIENTS
- bánh mì baguette
- smoked Lao pork sausage
- pickled carrot and cucumber
- coriander
- red curry jeow
- chilli crunch

It's said that the best Vietnamese cuisine outside of Vietnam can be found in Victoria, and it isn't uncommon to hear well-travelled Melburnians enthuse that, well, what they can get in their beloved city is even better. There are plenty of standout bánh mì shops offering superb sandwiches made with care in the city, and Ca Com is a relative newcomer, run by a pair of restaurateurs who wanted to give their own twist to the time-honoured flavours of Vietnamese bánh mì and Laotian khao jee pâté.

There's an innovative banhstrami (house-made pastrami layered with pickled mustard greens and dill) and a Lao Pork Sausage Bánh Mì humming with the flavours of galangal and lemongrass, alongside a generous stuffing of julienned vegetables, herbs and sauce, plus red curry paste and chilli crunch instead of pâté and fresh chilli. The superb flame-toasted bread (from a local specialist Vietnamese bakery) absorbs the flavours from the sandwich while maintaining structural integrity – no mean feat.

Despite that attention to detail, the price of bánh mì has become a battleground in the city for an inequitable perception held by some that Asian food should inherently be cheap – an outdated, racist attitude that devalues the labour and serves to dehumanize and marginalize the people and communities preparing it. That Ca Com and others charge their worth shouldn't be controversial – and especially when it's this good.

Conti Roll
(Re Store, Leederville, Perth)

INGREDIENTS
- crusty baguette
- assorted deli meats
- cheese
- pickles
- sun-dried tomatoes
- pickled aubergine
- roasted vegetables
- olives • a splash of Italian dressing

Indigenous Australians have seen a fair share of new arrivals on their land, and after the British, it is the Greeks and Italians who have had arguably the largest influence – at least on the nation's palates. Case in point: the Conti Roll (short for "continental"), a Western Australia variant of the Italian sub, forged in the kitchens of Perth and popularized by countless delis. It's a testament to the enduring legacy of Italian migration to the region and Re Store, established by Antonio and Gilda Re in the Leederville neighbourhood, has been a mainstay of their corner of Perth since 1936.

The Conti Roll was introduced as a way to showcase the deli's formidable array of imported Italian deli meats and cheeses, and to this day remains a harmonious blend of flavours and textures – crusty bread, a medley of deli meats (typically ham, mortadella and salami), complemented by slices of cheese, juicy tomatoes, tangy pickles, roasted vegetables and olives. The finishing touch is the store's signature Italian dressing, which ties all the elements together. In contrast to their minimal Italian cousins, which aim to showcase just a few ingredients at their peak, the Conti Roll's raison d'être is to almost kill you with generosity – literally the whole shop in a sandwich – and offer a riposte to the cliché "less is more".

Marrickville Pork Roll

(Sydney)

INGREDIENTS

- crusty baguette
- pork cold cuts
- pork pâté
- pickled and julienned carrot and daikon
- coriander
- chillies

As the Italian conti roll became an Australian culinary icon, so too has the pork roll, a casual simplification of the vibrant Vietnamese bánh mì, which has come to symbolize the best of what has thrust cities like Sydney and Melbourne into the culinary upper tier as food cities (spoiler alert: it's immigration).

In particular, the Sydney suburb of Marrickville has established itself as a stronghold of New South Wales' Vietnamese community, with one sandwich shop achieving near-mythical status: Marrickville Pork Roll. This Vietnamese-style bánh mì is a lesson in balance and flavour, featuring succulent slices of roast pork, cold cuts, tangy pickled carrots and daikon, fresh coriander, a generous smear of pâté, and a hint of chilli for heat. All of this is layered into a crisp, airy baguette that provides a satisfying crunch with each bite.

The story of Marrickville Pork Roll is deeply intertwined with the waves of Vietnamese immigration to Australia in the 1970s and '80s. Owners Khiem and Nga Du imported their culinary traditions to Sydney, setting up shop in the diverse and bustling neighbourhood. Their bánh mì quickly became a local favourite, drawing in a fiercely loyal crowd of regulars from all walks of life, who think nothing of travelling across the city for Nga's generously filled sandwiches, with its red-fronted signage a beacon on Illawarra Road.

Each ingredient in the Marrickville Pork Roll is chosen with the precision of a Swiss watchmaker. The pork is marinated and cooked to perfection, ensuring it's both flavourful and tender. The pickled vegetables add a necessary tang and crunch, complementing the richness of the pâté and the fresh brightness of the coriander. The baguette, baked daily, is the real MVP, providing the ideal vessel for this affordable and satisfying masterpiece.

While the city's bánh mì offerings have evolved since the shop's opening in 2008, it remains a cornerstone of the city's multicultural food scene, an emblem of soft power and culinary diplomacy that has paved the way for countless others.

Breakfast Muffin
(Hector's Deli, Melbourne)

INGREDIENTS
- English muffin
- egg
- sausage patty
- cheese slice
- Hectic sauce

Tucked away in Richmond, their original location, Hector's Deli has become perhaps *the* go-to spot for excellent gourmet sandwiches across Melbourne, but its breakfast muffin has a following all its own. Founded by Dom Wilton and Vanessa Bossio in 2017, the deli prides itself on fresh, high-quality ingredients, and you'll often find a line at the weekend. The breakfast muffin is a morning masterpiece, poetry in layers: a perfectly steamed egg, a sausage patty with the aniseed hum of fennel, melty cheese and Hectic sauce (their signature mildly spicy mayo with fresh herbs) all nestled within a griddled English muffin.

The sandwich shop is a cornerstone of Melbourne's legendary café culture, and embodies the locals' ability to take simple concepts and raise them to new heights. The muffin is a fast favourite for busy Melburnians, offering a satisfying start to the day – or a hangover pill, after a particular blurry night – that's straightforwardly delicious.

Credits

The publishers would like to thank the following sources for their kind permission to reproduce the pictures in this book.

Page 13 Jaz Ludwick; 16 Randy Duchaine / Alamy; 20 Steve Cukrov / Shutterstock; 23 William Morgan / Alamy; 28 The Photo Works / Alamy; 33 Tatiana Volgutova / Alamy; 37 Westmacott / Alamy; 57 Marc Guitard / Getty Images; 72 Yefim Bam / Alamy; 75 Jackie Ellis / Alamy; 82 Joe Cottington; 97 David Paw; 98 CCVectors / Stockimo / Alamy; 102 Schöning / ullstein bild / Getty Images; 126 Hector's Deli

All illustrations by Dave Bain.